CAMBODIA

THE ESSENTIAL GUIDE TO
CUSTOMS & CULTURE

KATE REAVILL

KUPERARD

"The real voyage of discovery consists not in seeking new landscapes, but in having new eyes."

Adapted from Marcel Proust, *Remembrance of Things Past*.

ISBN 978 1 78702 315 4

British Library Cataloguing in Publication Data
A CIP catalogue entry for this book is available
from the British Library

First published in Great Britain
by Kuperard, an imprint of Bravo Ltd
59 Hutton Grove, London N12 8DS
Tel: +44 (0) 20 8446 2440
www.culturesmart.co.uk
Inquiries: publicity@kuperard.co.uk

Design Bobby Birchall
Printed in Turkey by Elma Basim

The Culture Smart! series is continuing to expand.
All Culture Smart! guides are available as e-books, and many
as audio books. For further information and latest titles visit
www.culturesmart.co.uk

ABOUT THE AUTHOR

KATE REAVILL is a Cambodia-based writer, teacher, and travel photographer. Originally from Leicester, England, she is a graduate of the University of Warwick with a bachelor's degree in English Literature and trained as an English teacher at Oxford University. Kate has lived in Cambodia since 2018, after visiting the country on a month-long volunteer program, which precipitated a love and affinity for the land, its people, and their way of life. Today she is resident in the southern city of Kampot, where she teaches English and is an occasional presenter on Radio Oun, one of Cambodia's national radio networks.

CONTENTS

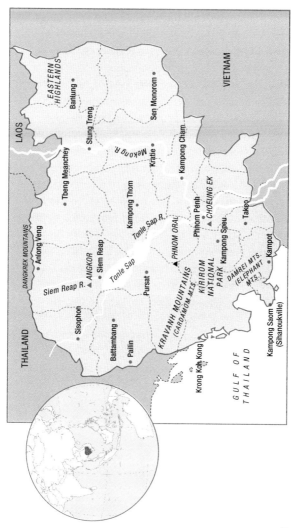

Say "Cambodia," and often two associations come to mind: the lost glories of Angkor, and the horrors of the Khmer Rouge. Any understanding of Cambodia today must embrace both these opposites, as well as the changing attitudes caused by technological development and something of a demographic revolution.

Cambodia was the center of the Khmer empire, which from its capital at Angkor from the ninth to the fourteenth centuries ruled much of what is now Vietnam, Laos, and Thailand. The ruins of the Khmers' palaces, temples, and cities testify to their power, wealth, high culture, and engineering skills, and their abandonment and long obscurity provide a sobering example of civilization's fragility. That one of the world's great civilizations arose here and left a heritage of such power and beauty is a source of great pride for Cambodians.

After the Thais captured Angkor in 1431, the Khmers moved their capital to Phnom Penh and maintained a precarious independence—a situation exploited by Portugal and Spain, until the expulsion of the Spanish in 1599. From 1600 the Thais and the Vietnamese vied for influence over Cambodia, beset as it was by rivalry within the royal family. In 1863 the French established themselves in Phnom Penh and brought Cambodia increasingly under their control. While retaining the trappings of monarchy, it became virtually a French colony.

During the Second World War, the Japanese occupation demolished French prestige. After the war,

Cambodian opposition and the conflict in Vietnam rendered the French position untenable, and in 1953 King Sihanouk declared Cambodia's independence, but the troubled years that followed culminated in the brutal regime of Pol Pot and the Khmer Rouge. In the 1970s an estimated one and a half million people were killed by execution, starvation, and forced labor. Those who survived carry with them memories and guilt. Young people, however, know only what they may have heard from their families: the subject is not openly discussed.

In the years since, Cambodia developed materially at considerable speed, and with one of the youngest populations in the world, attitudes that have been adhered to for centuries have begun to shift. In 2021, Cambodia carried out the fastest vaccination drive in all of Southeast Asia, and the country's close relationship with China has brought considerable and growing investment, but at a cost that makes some Cambodians uncomfortable.

Despite their traumatic past, Cambodians are courteous, hospitable, good-natured, and very welcoming—and they love a good party! Before the coronavirus pandemic, tourism was thriving, and, thankfully, has begun to pick up once more. Visitors to Cambodia can look forward to meeting some of the friendliest, most down-to-earth and resilient people in the region. Take the opportunity to learn about their history, traditions, customs, and way of life, and your trip will be greatly enriched.

Official Name	Kingdom of Cambodia	Preah Reacheanachakr Kampuchea
Capital City	Phnom Penh	Pop. 2.3 million approx.
Other Cities and Towns	Battambang; Kampot; Kampong Cham; Siem Reap; Kampong Saom (Sihanoukville); Kampong Thom; Sisophon; Takeo	
Area	69,990 sq. miles (181,040 sq. km), of which land 68,154 sq. miles (176,519 sq. km)	
Climate	Tropical. Wet monsoon season (May to October); dry season (November to March). Hot and humid; more moderate in the highlands.	Temperatures range from the high 70s°F (20s°C) in the cool season (December to January) to the high 90s°F (30s°C) in the hot season (April to May).
Population	17 million approx.	Growth rate: 1.3%
Ethnic Makeup	Khmer 97.5%; Cham 1.3%; Vietnamese 0.2%; Chinese 0.1%; other 0.9%	
Age Structure	0–14 years 30.9%; 15–64 years 64.2%; 65 years and above 4.9%	
Birthrate	22.02/1000; death rate 5.99/1000	

Language	Khmer	English and French are spoken in urban areas.
Adult Literacy	Approx. 81%	
Religion	Theravada Buddhism 95%; others (Christian, Muslim, animist) 5%	
Government	Multiparty democracy under a constitutional monarchy	Bicameral parliament consisting of the National Assembly and the Senate. Members of both houses serve 5-year terms.
Currency	The riel. 1 riel=100 sen	US dollars accepted. Thai Baht accepted in west of country.
Economy	Main exports include textiles, footwear, fish, and vehicles.	Main imports include fabrics, refined petroleum, vehicle parts.
Media	Seven TV stations, plus two relay stations for French and Vietnamese broadcasts	Khmer newspapers: *Reaksmei Kampuchea*, *Kaoh Santepheap*. English-language newspapers: *Cambodia Daily*, *Phnom Penh Post*
Electricity	220 volts, 50 Hz	Flat or round 2-pronged plugs
Internet Domain	.kh	
Telephone	The international dialing code is 855.	The code for Phnom Penh is 23.
Time Zone	GMT + 7 hours	

CHAPTER ONE

LAND & PEOPLE

*"When Angkorian society began, Paris and London
were not much more than elaborate villages. Europe
was crawling with barbarians, and here were the Khmer
engineering sophisticated irrigation systems
and constructing the biggest temple in the world."*

KIM FAY, THE MAP OF LOST MEMORIES

*"Once you've been to Cambodia, you'll never stop
wanting to beat Henry Kissinger to death
with your bare hands."*

ANTHONY BOURDAIN

GEOGRAPHY

Situated on the Indochinese peninsula, Cambodia,
roughly one-third the size of France, is bordered
by Thailand on the west, Thailand and Laos on the
north, Vietnam on the east, and the Gulf of Thailand
on the southwest. The Mekong River flows through

The "floating village" of Kompong Phluk, one of a handful of stilt-elevated villages on the Tonle Sap Lake.

eastern Cambodia from Laos in the north. At Phnom Penh, the capital, it divides into two courses, which exit through southern Vietnam to the South China Sea—a controversial domain in itself, which you'll come to understand more throughout this guide.

To the northwest of Phnom Penh is the vast Tonle Sap Lake, Cambodia's largest, which is linked to Phnom Penh and the Mekong River by a 100 km channel known as the Tonle Sap River. From November to April, Cambodia's dry season, the lake drains into the Mekong, but when the Mekong rises during the rainy season, water flows north from the Mekong filling the Tonle Sap. As a result, the lake's size, length, and water volume vary considerably over the course of the year. For centuries this phenomenon has created the great, low-lying

Wat Samprov Pam, situated on Bokor Mountain, which forms part of the Cardamom Mountain Range.

alluvial plain upon which most Cambodians live and which for centuries has been cultivated for rice, tobacco, corn, and fruit.

Today, the Tonle Sap is suffering the effects of upstream hydropower projects and dams, many of which are in China, as well as the effects of overfishing and drought. A fire during the 2016 dry season destroyed much of the lakebed forest, the natural habitat of the lake's freshwater fish, which forced many of the residents who live in villages floating on the lake to turn to land farming. It is not just the livelihoods of those who live on and around the lake that depend on the lake's continued health, however. The Tonle Sap provides around 60 percent of the entire country's protein intake in the form of fresh fish— its fate is of great consequence.

Surrounding the Tonle Sap is a large area of slightly higher plain rising to about 100 m, which supports woodland and grassland. Beyond this the country is bounded by high land: the Cardamom Mountains and the Elephant Mountains in the southwest, which include Cambodia's highest peak, Phnom Aoral, at 1,813 m and the Dangrek Mountains along the northern border with Thailand, marked by an east-west escarpment, 300 km long and rising to 500 m from the plain. The sparsely populated Eastern Highlands have both grasslands and deciduous forests while the highlands of the north and southwest have forests, ranging from tropical rainforest on the southwestern slopes to pine forests at higher

An aerial view of Kep province on Cambodia's south coast.

altitudes. The coastal strip has lowland evergreen forest on higher ground and mangroves along the coast.

Cambodia is a treasure trove of biodiversity and is home to hundreds of mammal, bird, fish, and reptile species, as well as more than 3,500 different plants, including the fragrant yellow and white Romduol, Cambodia's national flower. Sadly, many of these species are already suffering the effects of climate change, which are widespread and in recent years have become more tangible. The impact of climate change is also acutely felt by Cambodia's many subsistence farmers, who depend on regular and consistent seasons for their survival. Logging, mining, and the trafficking of animals have also taken their toll on Cambodia's natural environment. In an effort to protect the country's rich and diverse ecosystems, the government has increased its Protected Areas territory from 18 to 40 percent of total land area, though this, critics say, is not enough and that more action needs to be taken in order to prevent the rapid deforestation that is taking place.

CLIMATE

Cambodia's tropical climate has two main seasons: rainy and dry. The cool, dry, northeast monsoon from November to April is the perfect season for sun-worshipers, but the heat is often too intense, even for those Cambodians who are used to working in the fields. The warm, wet, southwest monsoon from May to early October brings strong winds and heavy rain, which can

cause devastating floods and ruin livelihoods.
However, when the rain does fall it usually comes in
the afternoon. Rainfall can vary from about 5,000 mm
on the slopes of the southwestern highlands to about
1,400 mm in the central plains. The annual flooding of
the Mekong deposits rich alluvial sediment that is critical
for the fertility of the central plain and provides natural
irrigation for rice cultivation.

The best time to visit Cambodia is between November
and April when the humidity is lower and there is
significantly less rain. Average temperatures in the
country range between 70°F and 90°F (21°C and 32°C).

THE PEOPLE

Cambodia's population is 97.5 percent Khmer, 1.3 percent
Cham, 0.2 percent Vietnamese, and 0.1 percent Chinese
(though there is also a large non-resident Chinese
population), while the remaining 0.9 percent is made
up of other ethnic groups, among them more than a dozen
indigenous hill tribes, such as the Kuy, Mnong, and Stieng,
who locally are referred to collectively as Khmer Loeu.

The Khmer were among the original inhabitants of the
flat, low-lying lands of the Mekong Basin. They mostly
practice Theravada Buddhism, and their language is the
official language of the country, spoken by 95 percent
of the population. Today, many people in the urban
and tourist areas also speak English, French, and more
recently Chinese, as a second or even third or fourth

language. The Vietnamese immigrated at different times during French colonial rule, some as minor officials and clerks in the colonial bureaucracy, others as laborers on the rubber plantations. Many were expelled by the Pol Pot regime and returned when Vietnamese forces overthrew the Khmer Rouge. Most have settled as rice farmers near the Vietnamese border, and there is a Vietnamese fishing community on the Tonle Sap Lake. Generally, they are among the less well-off.

The Chinese are relative newcomers to Cambodia and are predominantly employed in commerce, construction, banking, real estate, and trade. Chinese Cambodians suffered under the Khmer Rouge, but their expertise and connections have helped them to prosper in recent years as commerce and industry has increased under Prime Minister Hun Sen, and as a result of the Chinese Belt and Road Project. Since 2019, Cambodia has seen a remarkable boom in Chinese investment, though some of this concerns poorer Cambodians who have little or no property or financial rights, and so are often the collateral damage of vast development projects.

China is now Cambodia's biggest foreign investor, and despite the Covid-19-related lockdowns and associated economic slowdown, trade between the two countries reached all-time highs in 2021 with over US $11 billion traded, a 37 percent surge on the previous year. Despite an overall trade deficit with its northern partner, Cambodian exports to China also continue to grow and in 2021 they increased a substantial 39 percent on the previous year, with a total value of US $1.51 billion exported.

The Chams are a Muslim minority who came from the border region with Vietnam and whose ancestors once fought the Khmers and captured Angkor. Their language is related to Malay; they converted to Islam in the fourteenth century and adopted Islamic dress. They are located throughout Cambodia but are concentrated in Kampong Cham, the third biggest city in Cambodia, northeast of Phnom Penh.

In 2022, the overall literacy rate in Cambodia was approximately 81 percent, while life expectancy was seventy-two years on average (roughly sixty-nine years for men and seventy-three years for women). In the same year, more than 50 percent of the population was under twenty-two, a figure that bodes very well for Cambodia's economic future.

A BRIEF HISTORY

Archaeological research indicates that by 1000 BCE the inhabitants of the region were living much as they do today, in houses on stilts and eating rice and fish freshly caught in the river. The Mekong Basin was fertile and could support a large population—those whom we now know as the Khmer, who had their own language and prospered as farmers—while the Mekong River gave access to the sea and the fertile delta region. The different peoples began to coalesce into larger communities based on agriculture, crafts, and trade. As the population increased and trade and prosperity grew, so political centers developed and expanded to encompass weaker neighboring areas. The region became a transit for trade between India and China, Cambodia being a convenient stopping point.

Early Kingdoms

The first major state to emerge in the region was Funan, based in the Mekong Delta and lasting from the first to the sixth centuries CE. Much of the culture and many of the political institutions of succeeding Khmer states were derived from Funan. Funan itself was subsequently absorbed into the new state of Chenla, which had broken away from Funan in the mid-sixth century. In the late seventh century, Chenla was divided into north and south (land Chenla and water Chenla). Water Chenla had widespread maritime trade, reaching as far as modern Indonesia, but it was politically unstable and may have suffered a Javanese invasion. In troubled times an ambitious and capable man could establish himself as a political leader and dream of establishing his minor kingdom. By the end of the eighth century CE a Khmer kingdom had been

Depiction of a Funanese envoy to the Liang Dynasty in China.

established near the Tonle Sap Lake, and in 802 CE the prolonged period of Khmer political predominance and cultural splendor began, that came to an end only with the sacking of Angkor by the Thais in 1431.

The Khmer Empire

The ruler who inaugurated this period of Khmer predominance was Jayavarman II (802–50), who claimed descent from earlier rulers and had returned from exile in Java. On assuming power, and drawing on Hindu precedents, Jayavarman II instituted a new state religion with himself as Devaraja, or god-king. During his reign, he established himself at four capitals around the Tonle Sap, the last of which was 13 km from modern Siem Reap. Jayavarman II's new politico-religious system bolstered the ruler's prestige, power, and right to rule and demand obedience from his subjects. His nephew, Indravarman I (877–89), laid the economic foundations for Angkor's wealth and growth with a feat of hydraulic engineering remarkable for its size and precision, and making possible the irrigation and cultivation of large areas of land, extended even further by his successors, capable of supporting a large population in a relatively small area and providing the wealth and manpower for the emerging Khmer empire. Indravarman's successor, Yasovarman (889–910), seeking a site on which to celebrate his glory and prestige, moved the capital to the Angkor area, where it was to remain until the mid-fifteenth century.

The religion of the early Angkorian state was Hinduism, and the influence of southern India is evident in its architecture, sculpture, and political organization. Hinduism had flourished in the region for several centuries and was represented by the worship of Shiva and Vishnu embodied in a single deity known as Marinara. At the time of the move to Angkor, Shiva was the deity favored by the king, to be replaced in the twelfth century by Vishnu. The temples and shrines at Angkor are reflections in stone of Hindu cosmology, the central towers being representations of Mount Meru, the home

The Temple of Ankgkor Wat at Siem Reap. Originally a Hindu shrine, it was later converted to a Buddhist temple.

of the gods. Buddhism had also entered Cambodia by the first century CE and had coexisted with Hinduism, but it was not embraced by its rulers until the thirteenth century.

The Rise of Theravada Buddhism

During the thirteenth century, Hinduism gave way to Theravada Buddhism as the state religion, with Pali replacing Sanskrit as the sacred language at the beginning of the fourteenth century.

There are two major schools of Buddhism, known as the Theravada (Teaching of the Elders) School and the Mahayana (Great Vehicle) School. Theravada Buddhists regard their form as purer, reflecting more accurately the teachings of the Buddha. This form of Buddhism entered Cambodia through Southeast Asia from Southern India (it is often referred to as the "southern school"), whereas Mahayana Buddhism (also referred to as the "northern school") was carried through Nepal, Tibet, and China to Vietnam, and acquired accretions and practices that the Theravada Buddhists reject. Mahayana Buddhists refer to the Theravada school as the Hinayana ("lesser vehicle"), because of its more austere doctrine and practices.

The Decline of the Khmers

Over the following two centuries, Angkor fought wars against its Thai, Vietnamese, and Cham neighbors, the latter living in the area of south-central Vietnam. Fortunes wavered. The Chams, for example, defeated in the early twelfth century, rallied and inflicted a major defeat on the Khmers and occupied and sacked Angkor itself. They could not maintain their supremacy and were in turn defeated by Jayavarman VII (1181–1211), who built the new city of Angkor Thom, upon the walls of which the exploits of the king, including his defeat of the Chams on the Tonle Sap Lake, are vividly inscribed.

Over the next two hundred years, Khmer power slowly declined, partly because incursions by the Thais damaged the delicately balanced irrigation system. Consequently, the capital was moved to Phnom Penh in the mid-fifteenth century, after the Thais had once again captured Angkor. During the following century and a half, the Kingdom was weakened internally by dynastic rivalry and constantly threatened by the Thais to the west and, to a lesser extent, by the Vietnamese.

By this time, European powers were showing interest in the region. Spain established a presence in 1593, at first at the invitation of the king. This ended with the massacre of the Spanish garrison at Phnom Penh in 1599. Thereafter, a series of weak kings sought assistance against their dynastic rivals by allying themselves with either Thailand or Vietnam, until in 1863 King Norodom (1860–1904) signed an agreement making Cambodia a French protectorate.

Angkorian bust of Jayavarman VII, housed today in Guimet Museum, Paris.

In the 1860s France had acquired Cochin-China (southern Vietnam) as a colony. In 1884, it established protectorates over Annam and Tonkin (central and northern Vietnam). Finally, in 1887 it created the Union of Indochina, combining the four states under the overall authority of a governor-general. Laos was added in 1893.

THE "DISCOVERY" OF ANGKOR WAT

The French naturalist and explorer Henri Mouhot (1826–61) made four expeditions to the inner regions of Indochina, on the last of which he died, on November 10, 1861, in Laos. His diaries were returned to his wife and were published three times in quick succession. They appeared first in French, in magazine form, in 1863. In 1864 they were published in English in book form as *Travels in the Central Parts of Indochina (Siam), Cambodia, and Laos*. A French book edition was published in 1868. All these had engraved illustrations, many based on Mouhot's own drawings. A few European travelers had visited Angkor before and had written of it, but Mouhot's more detailed account and illustrations evoked a new interest, particularly in England and France. The time was ripe: the 1860s were witnessing a period of European imperial expansion, accompanied by intellectual curiosity and scientific research.

Mouhot's collection of specimens and descriptions of natural life were his principal interest. Nevertheless, he felt compelled to describe to the world Angkor, its ruins, and the civilization that it represented, and spoke of Angkor Wat as a temple to "rival that of Solomon, and erected by some ancient Michael Angelo," and as "grander than anything left to us by Greece or Rome," presenting "a sad contrast to the state of barbarism in which the nation is now plunged." But there was also another, more material, enticement to attract European attention: "Neither must I omit to mention the various productions which form so important a part of the riches of a nation, and which might be here cultivated in the greatest perfection. I would especially instance cotton, coffee, indigo, tobacco, and the mulberry, and such spices as nutmegs, cloves, and ginger—What might not be accomplished if these were colonies. . . governed as the dependencies of a great and generous nation." When the time came, that nation would be France, but Mouhot had brought Angkor into public consciousness in Europe, and that consciousness identified Cambodia as the home of Angkor—an identification that has persisted to the present and has become the basis of the Cambodian tourist industry today.

French Control

At first, the French protectorate had little impact on Cambodia's internal affairs, except to check further incursions from Thailand and Vietnam and protect King Norodom from his rivals. In 1870, however, the French forced King Norodom to sign a treaty that made Cambodia a French colony in all but name. This provoked a rebellion that lasted two years until the French agreed to revert to the pre-treaty situation. French control was gradually reasserted by agreement with Cambodian officials who saw advantages in acquiescing. In return the court was retained in splendor as the symbol of Cambodian sovereignty, and French pressure upon Thailand brought about the return of the northwestern provinces of Battambang and Siem Reap and the town of Sisophon to Cambodia in 1907. Thus, Angkor was again Cambodian. King Norodom was succeeded by Kings Sisowath (1904–27) and Monivong (1927–41). By the

A portait of King Norodom, taken in 1865 by Scottish photographer John Thompson.

time of the latter's death, the Japanese had occupied French Indochina.

Japanese Occupation

As servants of the wartime French Vichy government, the French colonial authorities remained in place and the French governor-general placed the eighteen-year-old Prince Sihanouk on the throne. However, under pressure from the Japanese, the French authorities returned most of Battambang and Siem Reap provinces to Thailand, which did not return them to Cambodian control until 1947. After the fall of the Vichy government in Paris toward the end of the war in Europe, the Japanese assumed control of the government of Cambodia, jailing the French administrators, until Japan itself surrendered and the French returned. The war period saw a great decline in French prestige and a relief to return to a slight "normalization" of Khmer national feeling.

Guerrilla War and Independence

After the defeat of Japan, Cambodia was granted autonomy within the French union, but the return to colonial rule was resented. Cambodian communists, influenced by the Viet Minh insurrection in Vietnam, began an armed resistance in the areas bordering Vietnam, while the Thais provided some assistance to Cambodian rebels on their border. The Khmer Issarak (Free Khmer) were little more than bands of guerrilla fighters, but the French were overstretched in Vietnam.

King Sihanouk at his coronation in 1941.

They had cloaked their control of Cambodia with the splendor of the royal court, thus enabling King Sihanouk to rally Khmer national feelings around the monarchy.

Facing opposition from the Democratic Party in Cambodia, King Sihanouk dissolved the Cambodian parliament in January 1953, declared martial law, and canvassed international support for full Cambodian independence, which he proclaimed in November 1953 and which was ratified by the Geneva Conference of May 1954 as part of the international agreements on Indochina.

To play a more active political role free of the restraints of monarchy, Sihanouk abdicated in favor of his father, Norodom Suramarit, in March 1955 and created his own political party. In the elections of September 1955, Sihanouk's People's Socialist Community (Sangkum Reastr Niyum) won every seat in parliament, giving him a democratic mandate. Sihanouk was prime minister until his father's death in 1960, when he became head

of state, retaining the title of Prince. Suspicious of
the policies of the United States, which supported
Thailand and South Vietnam, both of whom he
distrusted, Sihanouk declared Cambodia neutral
in international affairs. In May 1965, perceiving
plots against him by the United States, he broke off
diplomatic relations with Washington and inclined
toward Vietnam and China, turning a blind eye to
North Vietnamese and Vietcong use of Cambodian
territory as a sanctuary and supply route for their
forces in their conflict with South Vietnam and the
United States.

The Cambodian Civil War

Sihanouk's foreign and domestic policies alienated
both right and left wings of the Cambodian
political field. The urban elite and the officer corps
opposed his socialist economic policies and his
foreign policy, while many left-leaning educated
Cambodians resented the suppression of political
dissent. Widespread corruption was resented by all
classes, although Sihanouk himself enjoyed a semi-
divine status in the eyes of most of the population.
A Maoist-inspired rural rebellion in 1967 caused
Sihanouk to turn against the left. In 1968 the United
States began bombing inside Cambodian territory to
destroy Communist bases and disrupt their supply
lines, the Ho Chi Minh trail. These operations
developed into a carpet-bombing campaign that
killed thousands of Cambodian peasants created

a major refugee problem and turned more of the peasantry against the Americans and toward the Communists.

The Overthrow of Sihanouk

The conflict between the army and the rebels within Cambodia worsened, as Sihanouk's policy of neutrality had cut Cambodia off from United States aid, and his government's policy of nationalization alienated the middle classes and banking and commercial communities. While Sihanouk was abroad in March 1970, the pro-Western General Lon Nol and Prince Sisowath Matak deposed him and established the Khmer republic. Sihanouk set up a government-in-exile in Beijing. The political coalition he headed included a Cambodian revolutionary movement known as the Khmer Rouge, to which many Sihanouk supporters opposed to Lon Nol turned. Civil war broke out between the Khmer National Armed Forces (FANK) and the Cambodian People's National Liberation Armed Forces, which soon fell under the control of the Khmer Rouge.

In April 1970, US and South Vietnamese forces invaded Cambodia to expel the North Vietnamese from their bases, causing the North Vietnamese and Vietcong forces to retreat further into the country, increasing the threat to the corrupt, unpopular Lon Nol government. Chaos was unleashed as fighting erupted throughout the countryside and the US bombing campaign continued until August 1973, killing thousands and driving thousands more into Phnom Penh and other cities. The result was a surge of support for the Khmer Rouge.

Rise of the Khmer Rouge

Over this period, the Khmer Rouge, which had originally taken refuge in the countryside to escape Sihanouk's security forces, emerged as a dominant force under the leadership of Pol Pot (Saloth Sar) and Khieu Samphan. Lon Nol was regarded as a threat by the North Vietnamese and saw in the Khmer Rouge a force to be encouraged in opposition to Lon Nol. North Vietnamese forces entered northeast Cambodia, pushed out Lon Nol's troops, and provided training and arms to the Khmer Rouge, making them an effective military force. The most ideological, disciplined, and ruthless of the forces resisting the Lon Nol regime, they extended their dominance over other Cambodian opponents, including supporters of Sihanouk and those left-wing and communist elements influenced by North Vietnam or the Vietcong. As they recruited and indoctrinated fresh forces from the disaffected peasantry, the Khmer Rouge began to purge those they distrusted, including Cambodians who had received training in North Vietnam and those they suspected of attachment to Sihanouk. By early 1975, the Khmer Rouge was in control of the countryside and Phnom Penh was virtually isolated. Cambodia declared 1975 as "Year 0," supposedly a new beginning for what was yet to come.

THE KHMER ROUGE

The term "Khmer Rouge" (Red Cambodian) was first used by Prince Norodom Sihanouk in the 1960s to differentiate the left-wing Communist movement from the right-wing "Khmer Bleu." Almost undoubtedly the term "rouge" has connotations of bloodshed. Its leaders had become Marxists as students in Paris in the 1950s and had joined the French Communist Party. They had also acquired the intellectualism of revolutionary France and a belief that ideals could be realized if pursued and implemented with ruthless clarity. To bring about the ideal, in this case, the creation of a Communist peasant farming—or "agrarian"—society, any action was permissible.

This was an ideology and mindset alien to Cambodian social culture, yet perhaps there were some parallels with those absolute Angkorian monarchs of old who drove their people to great achievements, albeit in a much more creative and courageous way.

The Reign of Terror

Lon Nol fled in April 1975 and the Khmer Rouge seized Phnom Penh and immediately introduced a radical agrarian revolution. To completely restructure

Cambodian society they began a ruthless extermination of all possible opponents of their dream to build a Maoist, peasant-dominated, agrarian society. The cities were emptied, and some two million people, mainly from the educated and middle classes, were systematically killed. Creativity and imagination were frowned upon as these traits implied intelligence that could contradict and threaten the governmental ideals. Sihanouk, the nominal head of state, was removed from power. Cut off almost entirely from the outside world, Cambodia, now named Democratic Kampuchea, became a slave state.

A LEGACY OF LANDMINES

The reign of terror may be over, but it has left many problems for Cambodia. Notable examples of this are the unexploded landmines clustered predominantly in rural areas. Cambodia has almost the highest number of unexploded ordnance (UXO) in the world, with around 40,000 amputees suffering from Pol Pot's regime even now. Some estimates say that there are as many as 10 million landmines and UXO remaining. These have serious adverse effects on the agricultural industry and put a huge burden on poor families especially, those who are not able to afford treatment for injuries.

However, progress has been made to remove these landmines. In 2021, Kep, in the south of Cambodia, was named the first province to be landmine free, with all ten of its minefields cleared.

Vietnamese Invasion

In December 1978, responding to Cambodian incursions across their borders, the Vietnamese, in the name of the Kampuchean United Front for National Salvation, invaded and forced the remnants of the Khmer Rouge back to the jungles on the Thai border. Cambodia was renamed the People's Republic of Kampuchea and gained a new anti-Pol Pot communist government (PRK) headed by Heng Samrin. The country slowly began to rebuild itself under Vietnamese protection.

In the international climate of the day, the Vietnamese action did not meet with universal approval. The Soviet Union had supported the Vietnamese, but the Khmer Rouge in their Thailand refuge now received military aid from China. Royalist and republican groups also emerged. In June 1982 a coalition of all anti-Vietnamese factions was brought together under the auspices of the Association of Southeast Asian Nations (ASEAN) to create what was called the Coalition Government of Democratic Kampuchea to challenge the Vietnamese-backed regime in Phnom Penh. The coalition included the

Khmer Rouge. Faced with economic problems and the withdrawal of Soviet support, Vietnam withdrew its main forces in 1989.

Ceasefire and the United Nations Peace Process
In October 1991, the International Conference on Cambodia reached an accord (aka the Paris Peace Agreements) whereby the United Nations would take responsibility for implementing a peace plan leading to free general elections in 1993. In the interim, the different factions agreed to establish a Supreme National Council, under Prince Sihanouk's chairmanship, which would formally delegate powers to the United Nations Transitional Authority in Cambodia (UNTAC), including a supervisory role in administration and responsibilities for peacekeeping and conducting elections. The Khmer Rouge did not cooperate with UNTAC, refusing to disarm and stand down their forces or to permit access to their areas of control. On the other side, there was some intimidation by the government in Phnom Penh of a popular political faction led by Prince Sihanouk's eldest son, Prince Ranariddh. Despite tensions and fears of violence and a Khmer Rouge call for a boycott, the elections went ahead peacefully on May 23–29. There was allegedly a 90 percent turnout of the 4.6 million registered voters for the elections, which the United Nations Security Council deemed free and fair.

The Khmer Rouge had boycotted the elections, and elements in the army aided their resistance to the new government—an unstable coalition of Prince Ranariddh's National United Front for an Independent, Neutral, Peaceful and Cooperative Cambodia (FUNCINPEC) and Prime Minister Hun Sen's Cambodian People's Party (CPP).

The New Constitution

The elections enabled the drafting of a new constitution and the restoration of Norodom Sihanouk as a constitutional monarch. A government amnesty encouraged defections from the Khmer Rouge, which increased when the movement was outlawed in mid-1994. The coalition collapsed in violence in July 1997. Hun Sen emerged as sole leader, a position confirmed by the elections in mid-1998, despite complaints about electoral malpractice. Pol Pot died in April 1998 before he could be brought to trial, and the UN abandoned other war crime trials because of doubts about the integrity of the courts.

The Cambodian People's Party (CPP) won the elections in 2003 but did not find a coalition partner until June 2004. King Norodom Sihanouk abdicated in favor of his son, King Sihamoni, in October 2005. During 2006 Hun Sen reached a level of reconciliation with opposition leader Sam Rainsy of the Royalist party, FUNCINPEC, which was fraught with internal strife. While Cambodia conducted semi-competitive elections in the past, in 2018 the polls were held in a severely repressive environment. Since then, Hun Sen's government has maintained often violent and intimidating pressure on opposition party members, independent press outlets, and demonstrators.

Hun Sen is, as of this writing, the world's longest-serving prime minister, having taken office on January 14, 1985.

THE ECONOMY

Since 2010, Cambodia's economy has undergone a significant transition, reaching lower middle-income status in 2015 and aspiring to attain upper middle-income status by 2030. However, the impact of Covid-19 on the country has meant that the government had to dramatically downgrade its economic forecast, at least in the short term. Time will tell how quickly Cambodia can return to its positive long-term trajectory.

Chinese investment in particular has contributed to Cambodia's economy as a result of the deep-sea port in Sihanoukville which is part of a vital trade route for the Belt and Road initiative. The southern coast of Cambodia is now home to over US $5 billion worth of power plants and offshore oil operations, all owned by Chinese companies. While the government believes that its investment in agriculture and property development is positive, not everyone agrees. Some landowners are benefiting from an influx of unprecedented money, but many other locals either face eviction from their homes or land to make way for new projects. Some are simply driven out by the increasingly high cost of living. Tuk-tuk drivers are an example of the locals that are losing out, as their expenses have gone up, but earnings have gone down. As a result, many have no option but to move back to their villages and abandon life in the cities as rent prices have become unaffordable for many. However, the transformation has also brought employment to the city. Some Cambodians are finding more jobs available and can earn between US $120 and US $200 a month, which was a decent wage in 2022. In general, Cambodian workers on Chinese construction sites can often earn up to three times what they usually earn on local projects.

For centuries, Cambodia's economy has been based on agriculture, with most of the cultivated land devoted to growing rice and much of the remainder to rubber. In 2021, the Royal Government set a long-term development vision to modernize the agricultural industry. This move plays a key role in rendering Cambodia competitive, sustainable, and environmentally friendly.

The fishing sector has always been of major importance, much of it originally being based on the Tonle Sap Lake area. In 2021 a new initiative was introduced to set up an innovation nursery research team for aquaculture processing enterprises to address problems in the country's fishery industry.

On coming to power, the Khmer Rouge regime, for ideological and political reasons, was determined to make Cambodia self-sufficient. Thus began the forced exodus from cities and towns to provide labor for rice cultivation and large-scale irrigation projects. Private ownership of land was disallowed, all land was transferred to the state or state-run cooperatives, and industry was nationalized. The dispossession and execution of the educated and skilled classes removed those with the skills necessary to carry out and supervise the government's plans. The disruption was considerable and food was rationed and distributed by the state.

The Vietnamese-backed government of the People's Republic of Kampuchea, which took over in 1979, inherited a very battered economy requiring considerable reconstruction. Much of the infrastructure had been damaged or destroyed and famine was only averted with international food aid. As late as 1986, the government had to appeal to international agencies for rice. Nevertheless, by the mid-1980s the economy had returned to its healthy pre-1975 level, though there was still much needed in terms of reconstruction and attracting investment.

In 1989 the new anti-Vietnamese coalition government began to reverse the socialist policies it had inherited. Legislation was passed to restore the right to own and inherit property, denationalization began, and private enterprise was encouraged. A liberal investment code was introduced, the official currency rate was decontrolled, and restrictions on foreign trade were lifted. The impact of these reforms was felt first in Phnom Penh and the towns and did not impinge greatly upon the majority of workers who were employed in agriculture. Attempts to stabilize the riel failed until 1994, after a period when it had been withdrawn from circulation.

Economic reform and recovery were hastened by the presence of the UNTAC between 1991–93. The 22,000 United Nations personnel stationed in the country created a demand for consumer goods, which stimulated trade and investment, and was helped further when America lifted its trade embargo against Cambodia in January 1994.

The elections of 1993 brought FUNCINPEC into government, where it acquired the financial and economic portfolios. National budget and financial structure laws established central control of the economy. Tax, investment, banking, and currency laws were reformed and liberalized to encourage foreign investment and to provide protection against nationalization and guarantees of equal treatment with nationals, except in land ownership. Over the next few years, economic growth and levels of inflation fluctuated in response to external factors, but the overall trend was positive. The Asian financial crisis of 1998 combined with drought and internal political unrest caused problems, but Cambodia's admission to the Association of Southeast Asian Nations (ASEAN) in 1999 marked its full entry as a partner in the region.

The manufacturing side of the economy is led by textiles, which is growing once again following contraction due to pandemic-related supply chain issues—by the end of 2021 annual exports of garments and accessories from Cambodia increased by more than 15 percent. Cambodia has a wide range of minerals, including gold, bauxite, copper, tin, and zinc, along with granite and silicone sand. Since 2005 the government has tried to encourage increased foreign investment, with Australian mining companies showing particular interest and setting up joint venture projects to carry out exploration. After years of delays, in 2020 Cambodia began extracting crude oil from the Gulf of Thailand. The venture came to a halt when in 2021 the Singaporean operators filed for liquidation.

A major problem for the economy is the legacy of more than forty years of war and repression when a generation missed out on education and training. There is a shortage of skills, particularly in the countryside, and a lack of basic infrastructure in many areas. The challenge for the government is to encourage the private sector to address this disparity in cooperation with bilateral and multilateral donors such as the World Bank and the IMF.

COVID-19

Cambodia had a comparitavely slow start to the global pandemic. Cases were low initially, and throughout 2020 people walked around mask-free with no social distancing, lockdowns, or quarantine procedures in place. It was only in 2021 that substantial numbers of cases developed, which prompted authorities to accelerate measures to combat the disease. As case numbers rose, mass panic broke out and businesses were forced to comply with strict curfews, following restrictions imposed around the world a year earlier. The closures and restrictions had a huge impact on Cambodia's economy. People in designated "red zones" in Phnom Penh were at times unable to access food or medical assistance, and government aid was lacking. At the peak of the infection cases, hospitals were over-capacity, prompting authorities to set up temporary hospitals in stadiums, schools, and other public buildings. Though not ideal, it proved the government's willingness to take concrete and effective action to tackle the pandemic.

When Cambodia's first shipments of the vaccine arrived from China in February 2021, thanks in part to Prime Minister Hun Sen's close diplomatic relations with Chinese leader Xi Jinping, the country executed what has since been recognized as one of the most successful coronavirus vaccination programs in the world. By November the same year, Cambodia had double vaccinated approximately 80 percent of its population, earning it joint first position with Singapore in being the fastest vaccinating country in Asia—no small feat!

GOVERNMENT

Cambodia is a constitutional monarchy; the monarch is head of state, but the role, as defined by Cambodia's constitution, is entirely symbolic. Being one of the few elective monarchies in the world, Cambodia's king is elected by the Royal Throne Council, which consists of senior political and religious figures. The present monarch is King Norodom Sihamoni who rose to the throne on October 14, 2004, a week after the abdication of his father, Norodom Sihanouk. Except under the reign of the Khmer Rouge, a monarchy has been in existence in Cambodia since the first century CE and represents peace, stability, and the prosperity of the kingdom.

Constitutionally, Cambodia is a multiparty parliamentary democracy, though it has been dominated by one party since 1985. The head of government is a member of the majority party or coalition, named prime minister by the Chairman of the National Assembly, and appointed by the king. In 2022 the prime minister remains Hun Sen who, having held office since November 1985, is Cambodia's longest-serving head of government, and one of the longest-serving leaders in the world. The Council of Ministers, or cabinet, is appointed by the monarch on the advice of the prime minister. Elections are held every five years and there are no term limits.

Cambodia's bicameral parliament is made up of a National Assembly, consisting of 125 members of parliament who are elected to serve five-year terms, and the Senate, of which there are fifty-eight elected members who serve for six-year terms. Both the king and the National Assembly nominate a further two senators each, bringing the total number of senators to sixty-two.

CHAPTER TWO

VALUES & ATTITUDES

THE FAMILY

Cambodian people have a strong attachment to their community, village, and province, which they maintain throughout their lives. It is the family, though, that lies at the core of Cambodian society and is the main expression of group identity. Here, "family" means the extended family, and it's relied upon to provide safety, social security, status, occupation, and identity. In return, each family member is expected to fulfill their role and uphold the responsibilities defined by their position within the family unit.

In this collectivist society, social life also revolves around the family, and celebrations, whether for a wedding, birth, or some other occasion, are of great importance and are when bonds are reinforced. The institution of the family was a target of the Khmer Rouge and suffered severe disruption during that time. That difficult period saw family members turned against one another through indoctrination and fear. Those years hang like a shadow over many families, but the institution, and trust in its values, are being renewed as time passes.

Visit a Cambodian home and you may be surprised at the number of people you find there. There will be the nuclear family, which consists of a husband, wife, and children, plus often grandparents, uncles, aunts, nieces, nephews, and first cousins. In rural areas, if family members don't live under the same roof, they'll most likely live nearby.

Older family members are treated with respect and addressed with terms denoting their status. Thus, an older man will be addressed as *ta* (grandfather), *po*

A family relaxes together after a day of work in rural Siem Reap.

(uncle), or *boang* (brother); and an older woman will be addressed as *yeay* (grandmother), *ming* (aunt), or *boang srei* (sister). Younger children are referred to as *oun*. These terms are also used respectfully by people to address those who are not related to them.

Traditionally, the oldest male is considered to be the head of the household and expected to be the main breadwinner. The women of the household, meanwhile, are expected to fulfill the role of caregivers and home keepers, which includes taking charge of financial matters and the children's education. That is not to say that women are not also expected to work and make an economic contribution, but that this is expected to be secondary in importance. In recent years further shifts in these roles have taken place, particularly in urban areas, where the demarcation between male and female roles has diminished.

Among urban families, a new generation of educated women is challenging the traditional role of the husband. In addition, as individual agency becomes more important to young Khmer who are increasingly influenced by Western norms, the traditional arranged marriage has lost popularity.

Despite these changes, throughout Cambodia the traditional responsibilities and obligations between the generations prevail and continue to underpin family relations, with the young paying respect to their elders and providing care in their old age, and the elders extending care, protection, and love to the young.

CONSENSUS AND HARMONY

In addition to the importance of one's group identity are the notions of consensus and harmony, both of which are core values in Cambodia. As we've seen, Cambodia is a collectivist society, and great value is placed upon avoiding open conflict, which, rather than providing a solution, only causes all parties to lose face. Excessive displays of emotion are generally viewed as embarrassing by Cambodians who instead prize an ability to remain calm and control one's emotions and behavior.

A person who shouts or swears, makes threatening or derogatory gestures, or goes off in a huff and slams the door may express their feelings, but they'll also lose the respect of any Cambodians present. Instead, Cambodians use subtle and indirect means of communication to convey dissatisfaction, though, depending on one's place within the group hierarchy, no opinion or objection may be offered at all. Those perceived to be lower in the hierarchy, whether due to age or social rank, are expected to forgo their personal opinions in order to maintain external harmony and group cohesion. It is for this reason that some commentators in the West have argued that these values facilitate the creation of authoritarian states, in which the people defer to those who govern them in the name of the collective. Others see in these values a means of maintaining social order and harmony. Whatever your opinion on the matter, as a guest be aware that maintaining harmony and outward consensus trumps the individual's position on any given matter, and that going against this system is likely to cause difficulty.

COURTESY AND SAVING FACE

Good manners and propriety are highly valued in Cambodia, and a person who forgoes convention or acts rudely damages his or her own honor and reputation, as well as that of the person at the receiving end of their actions. Conversely, one's honor—that is to say, one's "face"—is maintained and added to by maintaining respectful behavior, complimenting, or supporting someone in some way, as all these gestures support a person's value and worth. As a form of social currency, face extends beyond the individual; the group with which one is most closely identified, usually one's family, is similarly damaged or bolstered by an individual member's actions and reputation.

What this means in practice is that it's important to be sensitive to how your words and actions come across—could they be taken as mockery or denigration, even if they are not intended as such, for example as when pointing out an error?

Because maintaining harmony is paramount and communication is often indirect and subtle, a Cambodian friend may well not tell you if you say or do something out of line, as doing so would cause you to lose face and disturb the harmony, superficial though it may be. Remember that under this system, passivity can be a form of action, and silence can speak volumes. Following common courtesies, many of which are described in this book, such as how to greet someone properly or what to be aware of when visiting a home as a guest, becomes easier with time, and the hints and subtleties others may use easier to pick up on.

Among younger Khmer, you will find that behavior is more relaxed, particularly if they have spent time abroad, and that as a guest to Cambodia the standards to which Cambodians are held in general will not be applied to you. However, any effort you make to adapt to the local way of doing things will be met with great appreciation and you will find that things become easier for you, whether you are in the country for only a couple of weeks, or a few years.

ATTITUDES TO TIME

Cambodians have a casual attitude to time, and in personal life particularly time is flexible. The casual approach is less marked in towns and cities, where business hours for government offices and companies provide a relative structure for the day. Even there, however, individuals may not be punctual in meeting those times. Shops can shut unexpectedly for hours, and so you'll find that patience in daily life is necessary.

In the world of religion, within the temples (pagodas) and monasteries (wats) set times for worship and prayer also provide structure. In the business world, those you work with will mostly be punctual. Government offices are less rigorous, however, and there is still the attitude that matters should take their course and time should be stretched to accommodate them.

A factor to bear in mind when it comes to timekeeping is that respect is based on age and seniority. As such, it is important not to keep an elder or superior waiting, because that would show disrespect. It would also show disrespect to bring a meeting with an elder or superior to a hasty end. When meeting a friend or colleague, allow plenty of time, and indicate at the start whether you are meeting anyone later that would mean having to run off by a certain time.

ATTITUDES TO OUTSIDERS

Cambodians are welcoming, polite, and easygoing, and generally will make allowances for the behavior of foreigners, who are usually referred to as *barang*. *Barang* means "French" in Khmer, but is used to refer to all foreigners. With the growth of the tourist industry and access to international media, there is now greater awareness of outside people and cultures.

Despite the trauma of recent decades, Cambodians are proud of their ancient culture and are anxious to retain their sense of identity as society modernizes. To that end, they will appreciate any effort you make to use their language, learn about their history and culture, and follow their etiquette.

Visitors should remember that the events that took place under the Khmer Rouge regime are not openly discussed. Those who survived the regime are burdened with their memories and younger people know only what they may have been told by their families. The generation still in power has retained certain tangible reminders, such as the Genocide Museum at Tuol Seng, where confessions were extracted under torture and the "Killing Fields" at Choeung Ek in Phnom Penh. As such, it's best to maintain sensitivity by not broaching the subject until your relationship with someone has developed sufficiently, and even then, to do so tactfully and in private.

ATTITUDES TO ASIAN NEIGHBORS

Cambodians' attitudes to their Asian neighbors are more complex. Over their long history, kept alive by the importance of Angkor and its monuments and art, the Khmers' relations with their neighbors have included both triumph and humiliation. We have seen in recent history how porous those borders are to incursions and how recently territories that now constitute the nation of Cambodia were in others' hands. Their relations with the Thais and Vietnamese have been the most complex, as explained in Chapter One.

Official relations between ASEAN nations, which is dedicated to mutual growth and development, are for the most part good, and most Cambodians would like to see their country's membership work to promote issues that are important to them, such as the health of the Mekong River, the environment, and food security. In recent years, however, some regional nations, including Cambodia, have come to increasingly regard ASEAN as being "slow and ineffective" and unable to cope with often fast-paced political and economic developments.

The mineral-rich waters of the South China Sea are the subject of a persisting dispute between China, regional countries, and the US and its allies. China has claimed "historical rights" over the islands, reefs, banks, and other features of the South China Sea, which is considered to be one of the busiest waterways in the world and is a significant gateway for trade and merchant shipping. Some ASEAN members are concerned that Cambodia could become "a proxy state" in the ongoing discussions about this shared maritime space between China and other global powers, including the US and Australia.

Having taken over the rotating chairmanship of ASEAN in 2022, Cambodia faces an uphill task to accelerate negotiations for a Code of Conduct in the South China Sea. Some see this as a crucial year for Phnom Penh to improve its international image, which was damaged when it was accused of siding with China and preventing ASEAN from reaching an agreement on the issue.

ATTITUDES TO MINORITIES

The political events of the past have impinged to some extent on the attitudes of ordinary Khmers, who retain some wariness toward Thai, Vietnamese, and Chinese people within Cambodia. The Chinese suffered persecution under both the Lon Nol and Khmer Rouge regimes. Lon Nol and his offices resented Chinese dominance in commerce and acted against the Chinese commercial class to further their own commercial and business interests. The Khmer Rouge persecuted all who were not rural peasants, and all Chinese, living as they did in the cities and towns, suffered. At present the Chinese who are Cambodian citizens are benefiting from the economic improvements and the government's improved relations with China.

Recent and ongoing Chinese investment in new national highways, international airports, and property development has caused a range of reactions among Cambodian citizens. While there has been an increase in certain jobs, such as construction work, rent prices have increased and numerous people have been bought out or evicted from their land to make way for new development projects. People have become concerned by the continually increasing deals between Cambodia's government and Chinese firms. The extent of investment and migration was such that Chinese nationals were bringing in their own taxis and street food carts, making it more difficult for local vendors to compete or benefit from the influx, and in 2019 a new law was introduced forbidding foreigners from owning and operating small businesses like these. Mining projects and government land concessions to foreign and local firms have also caused local residents to be displaced from their land.

Relations between Khmers and Cambodian Vietnamese are better now that their border conflict has ended, but the Vietnamese are generally looked down upon by the Khmer majority and are among the most disadvantaged in society. Relations with the few communities of Chams that still live in Cambodia appear to be good. Although the Chams practice Islam and retain their own sense of identity, the two communities coexist peacefully and, in general, there is not a great amount of intermingling between the two groups.

Cambodia's indigenous groups, known as Khmer Loeu, live in the mountainous northeast border regions and are generally little known by ordinary Cambodians. They are occasionally persecuted by their immediate neighbors and have also become the victims of exploitation of Cambodia's forest and mineral resources, though their plight has been largely ignored by wider society.

SAFETY AND CORRUPTION

Most expats would agree that Cambodia is a safe place to live and travel in, despite global assumptions that as a third-world country in Southeast Asia it may not be. As anywhere, though, it pays to be cautious, particularly in the run-up to public holidays when cases of petty crime tend to peak. When discussing the topic, one should bear in mind that accurate statistics on crime in Cambodia are non-existent. Filing a police report costs money and so many crimes go unreported.

Violent crime is rare in Cambodia, and even rarer does it involve foreigners. Expats and tourists can become the targets of pickpockets, however, and in general, walking around late at night alone is not advised. Away from the main streets, streetlights are few and far between, making it easier for crime to take place. Avoid exposing expensive jewelry on the street and keep your phone in your bag or pocket as it is easy for someone on a motorcycle to swipe it out of your hands. Extra care should be taken when crossing the road too, as hit-and-runs are sadly common.

Corruption in Cambodia is rife, with bribery in particular being a problem. An Anti-Corruption Law passed in 2010 that would see officials found guilty of corruption face up to fifteen years in prison is largely ignored and difficult to monitor since the police themselves are also known to accept bribes. During the coronavirus pandemic bribing became more common, with reports of officials accepting money so that individuals could avoid quarantine, illegally enter or leave the country, or to accept fake vaccination cards.

RELATIONSHIPS, DATING, AND SEX

As you might have guessed by now, sex is not a subject that is discussed openly in Cambodia, and protocol surrounding both sex and dating is quite conservative. In urban areas, with the advent of dating apps that allow people to interact more freely across social and class boundaries, it has become more common for younger men and women to date. In line with this development is the growing rejection of arranged marriages that were common in Cambodia's past, where parents would choose suitors for their children.

Both Cambodian men and women are quite romantic, as evidenced by the pop songs on the radio, music videos on television, and films, as well as from the sheer amount of heart emojis and GIFs shared on social media. Despite this, public displays of affection are highly inappropriate in Cambodia and so physical contact with a partner in public should be avoided, lest you embarrass anyone who happens to see you, as well as yourself. Among girls from more conservative backgrounds, it is quite common for a relative or friend to be brought on the date as a chaperone.

Virginity is highly valued and seen as a great virtue; in rural areas it is still the case that preserving virginity until marriage is a given and women who participate in pre-marital sex can be considered "ruined."

Prostitution, though illegal in Cambodia, is prevalent. Walking down the streets of most major cities—especially Phnom Penh—you will see a plethora of hostess bars, with scantily clad women standing outside inviting you inside. Drinks here will be expensive.

LGBTQ

Cambodia's LGBTQ community enjoys relative freedom and safety, though it does not yet enjoy full legal equality or social acceptance. Homosexuality is legal, indeed it has never been criminalized, and the age of consent is fifteen, regardless of orientation. Conversely, same-sex marriage is not currently legal (the government did accept recommendations by the UN to legalize same-sex marriage in 2019, but as of 2022 it had yet to be enacted), and legal protection in areas such as employment are lacking.

Social acceptance has increased in recent years, but discrimination and stigmatization persist, particularly in rural areas, where more conservative values prevail and forced marriages are not uncommon. Local cultural beliefs mean Cambodians can be more accepting of genders outside the binary of "men" and "women," as expressed by the Khmer term *khteuy*, which describes someone who was born into the gender of one body but identifies more with another gender. Today the term is usually used to describe men who identify as women. Depending on the context, it is also sometimes used pejoratively and so should not be used casually.

Overall, the situation is more positive in the cities, where there is a more visible LGBTQ presence, which includes coffee shops, bars, club nights, hotels, and an annual Pride parade, which has been held in Cambodia since 2003. The launching of *Q Magazine*,

Cambodia's first LGBTQ publication, in 2015, reflected the community's growth and increased public standing.

While sexual diversity has yet to be fully embraced, progress is being made, for example by NGOs like the Cambodian Center for Human Rights and Rainbow Community Kampuchea who campaign to advance legal equality and protection for LGBTQ Cambodians, as well as to improve education on gender and sexual diversity through the national school curriculum.

By and large, LGBTQ travelers will find a welcome environment in Cambodia, particularly in Phnom Penh and Siem Reap, where there are established gay scenes. As above, it is important to bear in mind that public displays of affection are considered inappropriate in Cambodia, regardless of orientation.

CHAPTER THREE

CUSTOMS & TRADITIONS

RELIGIONS OF CAMBODIA

Cambodia has a rich religious tradition. About 95 percent of Cambodians practice Theravada Buddhism, the state religion since the thirteenth century, except for during the Khmer Rouge period. This was due to the massacre of monks and religious scholars who, if not murdered, were forced into exile. The remaining 5 percent are Cham Muslims, Christians, and animists. There is also an increasing number of Western and Chinese religions being practiced throughout Cambodia.

Before the thirteenth century, Hinduism was one of the Khmer Empire's official religions, which can be seen in the iconography at Angor Wat, the world's largest Hindu temple and one of the only temples dedicated to Brahma. The most revered Hindu deities were Shiva and Vishnu, for a time embodied together in the form of a single deity known as Marinara. The kings of the early Angkor period favored Shiva, superseded by Vishnu in the twelfth century.

In the thirteenth and fourteenth centuries, Theravada Buddhism became firmly established, having entered Cambodia from India through Southeast Asia. The changes in religious allegiance are demarcated in the temples and shrines at Angkor. Despite the triumph of Buddhism, however, elements of Hinduism survived and are still present in the rituals and customs associated with those fundamental rites of passage of birth, marriage, and death.

Theravada Buddhism teaches the concept of nirvana, or extinction of all desire and suffering to arrive at the final level of reincarnation, while the "Five Precepts of Buddhism" prohibit drinking, killing, stealing, fornication, and lying. In daily life, Cambodians will make their own judgment on what rules to follow and to what extent. More uniformly practiced is the celebration of major Buddhist holidays, such as Pchum Ben (Ancestor's Day), when locals flock to pagodas to make offerings.

Traditionally, all young men were expected to become monks, but the time spent as a monk has for most been reduced to a token fifteen days, and sometimes less. Today less than 5 percent of men become monks, compared to nearly 100 percent a century ago. Often the reasons for becoming a monk are due to receiving an education which their families may not be able to afford or to lessen the burden on families with too many mouths to feed. While living according to the strict routine of the monastery, monks can also be seen in shopping malls and restaurants. Overall, Buddhism remains a potent force in society,

A Buddhist monk blesses worshipers.

having survived the widespread destruction and killings of the Khmer Rouge to be reinstated as the state religion.

Islam is the religion of the descendants of the Chams, who migrated from Vietnam after the defeat of Champa by the Vietnamese in 1472. Among Cham Muslims, the call to prayer is the beating of a drum, as is done by Buddhists.

Christianity was introduced with limited success by the French and made some headway in the cities, particularly Phnom Penh. Christians also suffered under the Khmer Rouge, though they have made a comeback with the growth of communities around the country. Still, they remain a small minority.

Animism and Folk Traditions

Animistic beliefs and folk traditions run parallel with religion in terms of importance to Khmer people, who long before the introduction of Hinduism and Buddhism believed that all things have a spirit or soul, including

Spirit houses are commonly found in Cambodia and are created to honor and placate local spirits that may be present.

animals, plants, rivers, mountains, stars, the moon, and the sun, and that these spirits had to be placated and venerated. These beliefs are still widely held today, though they have largely been subsumed into the prevailing Buddhist faith, despite the seeming dissonance with traditional Buddhist belief, which sought to subdue the chaotic world of spirits and the supernatural.

In its purest form, animist belief and practices are still found among the Khmer Loeu, the collective name given to Cambodia's indigenous groups that reside in the country's highlands, such as the Bunong, Tampuan, and Koy. Numerous traditions persist among the wider population, too. For example, many Cambodians believe that spirits of the departed inhabit their familiar surroundings even after death, awaiting their transition to the next life. As such, spirit houses are erected to placate these spirits, especially if their familiar surroundings have been altered. When a new house is built or a new building is erected a spirit house is provided to house the disinherited spirits, usually at a little distance from the new building. Cambodians will offer gifts of flowers, incense, food, and drink to the spirits, to placate them and to seek their blessing.

In addition, blessings from monks are given before new businesses open to ensure the success of the venture and protect against evil. Fortune tellers are important figures for Cambodians and are consulted about important decisions such as marriages, building a new house, or going on a long journey—among other things.

Young children release caged songbirds for a small sum of riel for good luck and prosperity.

Beliefs in evil and malicious spirits that bring misfortune and sickness also persist. Certain plants are thought to deter them, as is having a raised doorstep or a carved figure to ward them off. Incense sticks may also be lit to ward off evil spirits and protect the property and the people inside it.

COVID-FIGHTING SCARECROWS

In one particularly modern example of animist belief and practice, during the coronavirus pandemic, scarecrow-like effigies dressed up in everything from dresses to spacesuits were erected outside homes and villages around the country to ward off the disease, and bonfires were lit. At the time Prime Minister Hun Sen issued a statement against the supernatural scarecrows, known as *ting mong*, saying that people shouldn't rely on superstition to fight the pandemic and that the situation had become risky as the scarecrows and bonfires constituted major fire hazards, especially during the dry season. This did little to diminish people's belief in their efficacy, however.

FESTIVALS AND NATIONAL CELEBRATIONS

Festivals are celebrated according to the lunar calendar, and thus the corresponding dates in the Gregorian calendar change from year to year. They are in most cases also public holidays. Diaries published in Cambodia give the dates for each lunar festival, and the dates of the public holidays linked to them.

In 2020, the government reduced the number of public holidays from twenty-eight to twenty-two in an attempt to increase competitiveness and productivity, but the decision was met with much disapproval as some thought it was damaging to workforce morale and the celebration of cultural heritage. Despite the reduction, Cambodians still enjoy far more public holidays than most countries.

If the dates for a public holiday fall on a weekend, the holiday is taken during the following week. Some Cambodians will also be given a short period of time off work during major festivals and celebrations. Public holidays are taken very seriously in Cambodia; families spend time together, and pagodas, in particular, are visited. At larger festivals, firework displays are common, and you might find that you get soaked by a water gun—children love to run around squirting water at people!

Chaul Chnam Chen (Lunar New Year)

Ethnic Chinese and Vietnamese celebrate this festival in late January or early February. The festival lasts about fifteen days, with the first and last days being the most publicly celebrated. Chinese and Vietnamese shops close for at least part of the time, and family and friends visit one another. If invited to the house of a friend or colleague, take a small gift of money for the children (in Chinese an *ang pau*). *Ang pau* envelopes are available at Chinese stores, and the gift should consist of new notes. Dress should be smart and conservative on such occasions. Most people wear red, as this symbolizes

good fortune. Generally, men are not required to wear
a tie but seek advice on proper attire from Chinese and
Vietnamese friends and colleagues or expats with some
experience. If you are visiting Chinese and Vietnamese
friends or the home of an employee, "smart casual"
would apply.

Bon Chaul Chhnam (Khmer New Year)

This is celebrated for three days on the thirteenth or
fourteenth of April each year and celebrates the end
of the harvest season. It is Cambodia's single most
important holiday and shops close, cities shut down, and
people return to their provinces. Typically, there will be
parties, visits to the local pagoda, and most importantly,

Dancers celebrate Bon Chaul Chhnam at Angkor Wat.

time to spend with family and friends. It is customary to allow employees to take time off work.

Chat Preah Nenkal (Royal Plowing Festival)

This solemn occasion usually takes place in early May (Pisak) and is held to mark the start of the rice-growing season and the end of the dry season. Proceedings are usually led by the king and there are feasts and prayers for a plentiful crop. Plates of food are prepared to represent the various crops of Cambodia. However, the highlight of the festivities is undoubtedly the ceremony that takes place in front of the National Museum, next to the Royal Palace. Usapheak Reach (the Royal Oxen) is a crucial part of the event, as they begin plowing and monks scatter rice. It is believed that the Royal Oxen play an important role in determining the fate of the coming agricultural harvest.

King Norodom Sihamoni at the Char Preah Nenkal ceremony, Pnomh Penh.

Visaka Puja

Falling on the eighth day of the fourth moon in May or June, Visaka Puja celebrates Buddha's birth, enlightenment, and death. Candlelit processions of monks take place at wats and pagodas across the country, with the most evocative at Angkor Wat.

Pchum Ben (Ancestor's Day)

This fifteen-day festival is another significant religious holiday in Cambodia, falling between mid-September and early October and culminating in celebrations on the fifteenth day of the tenth month in the Khmer calendar at the end of Vassa (Buddhist Lent). During Pchum Ben, Cambodians traditionally wear white and make offerings of food and drink. These contributions to the monks at the pagodas are thought to benefit the departed ancestors who are said to be especially active at this time of year.

Bon Om Tuk (Water Festival)

In early November, Bon Om Tuk celebrates the naval victory of Jayavarman VII over the Chams in 1181, and marks the end of the wet season, and showcases the unique reversal of the Tonle Sap River current. It also coincides with the so-called "Harvest Moon," the time when rice crops are meant to be at their peak. Tonle Sap is the only river in the world that can claim this unusual characteristic and for three days, locals and expats travel to Phnom Penh to enjoy the colorful boat races, extravagant firework displays, and many other celebrations that see millions of people lining the streets.

A rowing team takes part in the traditional Bon Om Tuk boat race on the Tonle Sap River.

Victory Over Genocide Day

Also known as Cambodian Victory Day, this day marks the overthrow of Pol Pot and the end of rule by the Khmer Rouge in 1979. The public holiday is a solemn affair as it commemorates such a distressingly dark period in history for Cambodian people and is a day to remember all those who lost their lives. Not all partake in the commemorative services as many Cambodians feel uneasy about their dependence on Vietnam for liberation and the ten-year long occupation by Vietnam that followed.

PUBLIC HOLIDAYS

These are state holidays, dated according to the Gregorian calendar, and include internationally recognized observances and anniversaries of events relating to the Cambodian state and its history.

As with other festivals, if the dates for a public holiday fall on a weekend, the holiday is taken during the following week.

January 1	International New Year's Day
January 7	Victory over Genocide Day
February	Lunar (Chinese) New Year
March 8	International Women's Day
Mid-April	Khmer New Year
Late April	Royal Plowing Day
May 1	International Labor Day
May 13-15	King Sihamoni's Birthday
May 20	National Remembrance Day
June 1	International Children's Day
June 18	Queen Mother's Birthday
September 24	Constitution Day
Early October	Pchum Ben
October 25	Paris Peace Agreements Day
October 31	Commemoration of the King's Father
November 9	Independence Day
Mid-November	Bon Om Touk

RITES OF PASSAGE

Birth, marriage, and death are universally recognized rites of passage in Cambodia and are highly important and often expensive affairs. Many of the practices surrounding birth, marriage, and death are cultural rather than specific to Buddhism.

Birth

The birth of a child is a significant and welcome event. Traditionally a woman is assisted by a birth attendant or midwife, usually an older woman who had learned from attending births within the family or within her community. This practice persists in rural communities, but these days most will have received some training in hygiene and basic awareness of possible complications that may require referral to a clinic or hospital. In urban areas, women have access to a hospital or clinic providing proper neonatal and pediatric medical attention.

Traditionally, Cambodians believed that a woman's body must be warmed after the birth, as must the baby, often referred to as "roasting." After the birth, the baby was wrapped in cloth and the woman covered. A common practice was for the mother and baby to lie on a bed above or close to a fire for up to a week. During this time the woman might be sponged with warm water, but may not wash or shower in cold water. One practice included the woman sitting on a fire-warmed stone, or lying with such a stone on her abdomen. Another involved steaming, where the woman was encouraged to sweat out impurities over steam from boiling water containing a mixture of herbs, during or after which she might apply a pounded mixture of galangal and turmeric root to her body. These practices were said to make the uterus shrink, prevent sagging of the stomach, and combat illness.

During and after pregnancy, women were encouraged to eat spicy food, such as pork or fish prepared and cooked with black pepper and ginger, and to drink large quantities of a concoction of herbs boiled in water with rice wine. Nowadays the recommendation for all pregnant women is to consume as much calcium as possible, to keep both themselves and their babies healthy.

Whatever the medicinal virtues of this traditional regime, it also served the purpose of ensuring the woman had a period of rest and attention after the birth and time to devote to the baby, before returning to the realities of what for many is still a hard existence.

Today these traditional practices are less observed or have been adapted depending on access to modern medical procedures. However, many medical personnel died under the Khmer Rouge regime and training of healthcare professionals was interrupted, so there is a shortage of trained midwives—a situation that the government is trying to remedy. Meanwhile, although traditional midwives have received basic training in modern midwifery practice, the old ideas, like "roasting," die hard. In the past, expats may have avoided Cambodia as an unsafe place to give birth, but increasingly fears are abating due to modern facilities in hospitals such as the Royal Phnom Penh Hospital, and today infant mortality rates are lower across the country than they ever have been.

"Crossing the river" (*chlong tonlee*), is a metaphor used by elderly Cambodians to describe the process of giving birth, comparing it to the difficulty and danger of crossing the Tonle Sap.

Marriage

Marriage in Cambodia is an important life event and is celebrated as extravagantly as the family can afford. Traditionally marriages were arranged, and while this does still occur in more rural areas, young Cambodians in the cities are more likely to choose their spouse out of love and personal choice, rather than wealth, status, or convenience. Most Khmer are under pressure to marry by the age of twenty-five, and it is rare for women to remain single long after this.

Where arranged marriages do occur, partners are often found from different branches of large extended families, though marriage between close blood relatives is forbidden. In the past, it was not unusual for parents to keep an eye out for suitable partners for their children and make contact through a go-between with the other family so that an understanding may be arrived at while the proposed partners are young.

The Ceremony

The traditional Khmer wedding ceremony symbolically recreates the marriage of Preah Thong, the first Khmer ruler, to the Naga princess Neang Neak. According to legend, Preah Thong was wandering in exile from his homeland when he met and fell in love with Neang Neak. Her father sanctioned the marriage and, as a gift to the happy couple, swallowed a part of the ocean and thus created the land of Cambodia. A Khmer wedding, therefore, has all the splendor and ceremony of a royal wedding, with the groom and his bride dressed as royalty, being prince and princess for the day. Family, friends, and other members of the community join in, and musicians perform on traditional instruments.

Weddings take a lot of organizing in Cambodia, and unlike in the Western world, the guest list is less stringent, with people invited by association or people that the couple has only met a handful of times. The idea is to make them as large and impressive as possible. Weddings can last anywhere between twenty-four hours and three days, depending on the wealth of the family, and usually start very early in the morning and continue until late.

The wedding season typically starts in October when huge tents take over the streets celebrating the new unions. In the morning the groom and his family and friends go in noisy procession to the home of the bride, bearing wrapped platters of fruit and Khmer desserts. There they are met by a representative of the bride's family, who inspects the gifts and, if of sufficient quality and quantity, begins a humorous verbal exchange with

The groom and his family begin their procession to the home of the bride.

the representative of the groom, which ends with the groom and his followers being invited into the bride's home.

The couple is then blessed by three, five, or sometimes seven monks, before undergoing an elaborate cleansing ceremony during which the parents of the bride and groom and their relatives and friends take turns to symbolically cut the hair of the couple and wish them well. Following the hair-cutting ceremony, married couples form a circle around the bride and groom; three candles are lit and passed around the circle clockwise seven times, each person passing his or her hand over the flame in a sweeping motion toward the couple as a silent blessing. Only married couples may participate because it is believed that they will pass on to the bride and groom the secret quality that has preserved their union. The bride and groom are seated for the ceremony, in which the spirits of the ancestors of the two families are invoked, and all those present are invited to observe and bless the wedding. The only silent part of the ceremony is when the couple is blessed by monks.

Most weddings include traditional ceremonies with stories about ancient Khmer myths organized in a specific order and are followed by a sit-down dinner and plenty of drinking. Cambodians notoriously encourage everyone to drink by clinking glasses before every sip and saying "*choul muoy*!" There will be entertainment and lots of dancing—Cambodians love to dance—and most likely karaoke, another favorite at any wedding.

Dress codes are becoming more relaxed but most Cambodian women will still wear traditional dress and have "wedding make-up and hair" done at a salon beforehand.

In the cities and among the wealthier members of society, the postnuptial celebration is held in a restaurant. In the rural areas, poorer families get together to organize the celebration, erecting awnings and preparing food.

If you are invited to a wedding, ask a Cambodian friend what to expect. Customs are changing, especially in the cities, although the traditional pattern remains.

Attending a wedding comes at a cost, however. In your invitation, you will be provided with an envelope to discreetly deposit money as a gift to help cover the costs of the occasion. The amount you offer is up to personal choice and financial means, but a minimum of US $20 is usually an acceptable amount.

Mixed foreigner-Khmer marriages are increasingly common, and these usually consist of an older Western man with a younger Khmer woman. Sometimes this is out of love, but often is complemented by the financial support that the *barang* can offer the Khmer woman and her family.

Death

While grief is felt and expressed at death, it is tempered among the Buddhist Khmer by the belief that it is not only the end of this life but the beginning of another, better life. After death, the body is washed, dressed, and placed in a coffin, which is usually decorated with flowers and displays a photograph of the deceased. Bodies will typically only be kept for three days, and monks will come and recite sermons each evening by the body. White pennants, known as white crocodile flags, are hung outside the house to signify that a death has taken place. Chanting and mourning music, nowadays often amplified and beginning as early as 4:30 a.m., is played during the mourning period, which may last for one or two days. The procession to the temple for cremation is accompanied by an *achar*, or master of ceremony, and is made up of Buddhist monks, members of the family, and other mourners. There must be no animals present as if they make a noise, this is assumed to become attached to the soul of the deceased forevermore. It is also frowned upon for women to wear make-up, as this is seen as disrespectful to the deceased's family. After the cremation, relics of the dead such as teeth and fragments of bone are often collected to be worn on gold chains as amulets.

CHAPTER FOUR

MAKING FRIENDS

"The most beautiful thing in Cambodia isn't the country, it's the Cambodian people."

RITHY PANH, CAMBODIAN DIRECTOR
AND SCREENWRITER

Moving to a place where you have no friends or family can be daunting, but Cambodia is as welcoming a country as you can find. So much so in fact that in 2021 it was ranked the friendliest country in Southeast Asia by Rough Guides. Striking up a conversation is easy; Cambodians love practicing their English and appreciate it when foreigners attempt to speak their language too, even if those attempts are not always successful. As a result, acquaintances in Cambodia are easy to come by and indeed are useful to have. Developing more meaningful friendships, however, is harder, and while not impossible, requires both an investment of time and at least a basic grasp of Khmer. The effort though is worthwhile. You'll find your

Cambodian friends to be loyal, considerate, reliable, and great company, and the friendships you'll make will greatly enrich your time spent in the country.

MAKING CONNECTIONS

Most Cambodians make their friends through family connections and in school. In rural areas, children come together to go fishing, play in the field, or in the floods during the rainy season, and share food together. In the cities, there are more activities and social events for young people to meet each other and form friendships.

Despite the obvious language barrier, many Cambodians will want to try to converse with you and learn more about you. Happily, the benefits of befriending Cambodians far outweigh the struggles of communication. Not only will you enjoy their good company, but you will also develop useful connections and, hopefully, get to see a side to the Kingdom of Wonder beyond the museums, ruins, and beach resorts.

Whether you are out for a meal or enjoying a drink, you will find locals to be interested and open to conversation. Get talking to people and try out a few Khmer phrases—you'll soon be invited to come back. If you are invited to have some food or to go to an event, you will be expected to attend. Whereas sometimes *barang* (foreigners) might use throwaway terms like say "see you later" or "maybe come for a drink tonight," Khmer take these suggestions more literally.

First encounters can be intimidating, particularly for locals who may speak little English. Always smile and say "Hello" (*Susaday*). There is more information on greetings below and in Chapter Nine.

If you are staying in Cambodia long term and find yourself in need of company, you could join one of the many local Facebook groups. Popular groups include Expats in Cambodia, Cambodia Backpacker Travelers/Tips, Phnom Penh Expats, and Inside Cambodia, to name a few. There is a multitude of groups to choose from in the cities that will help you learn more about where things are happening and where you can meet other expats and locals.

Those in the capital are spoiled for choice. You can socialize while keeping fit by joining the Phnom Penh Easy Riders bicycling group, which has run Saturday morning bike rides around Phnom Penh since 2005. The rides usually leave at 6:30 a.m. and finish somewhere between 11:00 a.m. and 2:00 p.m., depending on length. While the pace is medium the length of the rides is relatively long, usually between 35 and 60 kilometers. A coffee and food break is taken in the middle of the ride.

If you speak French, you can join the Francophones a Phnom Penh Group, which is frequently updated and has more than four thousand followers who meet up and exchange tips and tricks about expat life in Cambodia. Enjoy listening to or playing music? Join the Phnom Penh Musician's Collective, a friendly group that organizes events to help musicians to meet each other, collaborate, share their music, and form bands. If you want to know what's happening at night and where you can let your hair down, check the Nightlife Phnom Penh Facebook group which is updated daily with the latest deals and events at bars, clubs, restaurants, and pop-ups.

The Expats in Cambodia online forum has an enormous amount of information from other expats and often promotes social events.

Social media plays a huge part in the upkeep of friendships today, and a lot of interaction takes place online. As such, don't be offended if you are sitting with your new local friends and they are glued to their smartphones—for better or worse, it is now considered normal.

GREETING

In general, behavior in Cambodia is governed by the factors discussed earlier in the book: showing respect, observing the social hierarchy by deferring to age and position, behaving and dressing modestly, and maintaining harmony by avoiding confrontation with politeness and good manners. In all social situations, it's a good idea to find out, whenever possible, the age, status, and relationship of those present so that you know how to greet them appropriately. As we saw in Chapter Two, an older person could be referred to as *ta*, *po*, or *boang* if they are male, *yeay*, *ming*, or *boang srei* if they are female, and if the person is younger than you, by using *oun*. So don't be perturbed if someone asks your age well before asking your name; asking your age is simply to find out whether you are older than they are so they can greet you properly.

The traditional greeting in Cambodia is the *sompeah*, in which the palms are held together as in prayer while bowing slightly. The higher the hands are lifted and the lower the bow, the greater degree of respect the greeting communicates. About chest to neck height is appropriate for someone of equal age or standing, as it is for a younger person too. If greeting an elder or someone of importance, such as a teacher or a monk, your hands should be lifted to between your nose and forehead. It is bad form when greeting someone of lower age or social rank to lift your hands too high as this can cause the other person some embarrassment. The person who is younger or lower in rank is expected to greet first, to which the other person is expected to respond.

It is only necessary to *sompeah* on first meeting someone or when seeing someone you have not seen for a while. If the meeting is a formal one, while performing the *sompeah* you should say, "*Choum reeup sooa*," and on departing perform the *sompeah*, and say, "*Chum reeup lear*."

When meeting, if you are wearing a hat, it is polite to remove the hat and bow your head. The head is regarded as the center of intelligence and spirituality. As such it is sacred. By bowing the head, a person shows respect.

The more informal everyday greeting is to simply say "*Susaday,*" without a *sompeah.* In cities and tourist areas where Western influence is more marked, handshaking has become common between men, but women are more reluctant, out of modesty, to shake hands, particularly with men.

DRESS

In tourist areas, Cambodians tolerate standards of dress that they would otherwise regard with some disdain. Most Cambodian women dress very conservatively and keep their shoulders and knees covered by wearing long sleeves and long skirts. In bigger towns and cities, Western dress is common. Many women and children also wear pajamas during the day as they are light and comfortable. Swim shorts and going bare-chested is acceptable only at beach areas, and is unacceptable in wats and pagodas. If you have come to Cambodia for work, you will find that dress in the workplace is much as you are used to. Offices are usually air-conditioned.

INVITATIONS HOME

If you are resident in the country for any length of time, you will meet Cambodians who will invite you home for a meal. In a family context, you will be introduced to the older members of the family first, and if they are older than you, you should be the first to perform the *sompeah*. If there are family members younger than you, they will greet you after their elders and perform the *sompeah*, to which you may respond with the same gesture or a bow of the head. If you are a guest more often, then the same pattern will apply but the gestures may be less formal.

More commonly, you will be invited to meet in a restaurant. At other times you may meet informally, or perhaps accidentally, in a public place. The following points of etiquette should help you avoid embarrassment whatever the circumstances.

As a guest at a family occasion be sure to be as respectful, polite, and grateful as possible. Try not to reject food or drink as it can seem insulting. If offered alcohol, you will quickly realize that this is a time-consuming affair, as the Cambodian people love to say "cheers" every time they take a sip, especially when *barang* are present. It is advisable to only drink when others do! To say cheers, you shout "*choul mouy*"— which translates directly as "bump one."

DOS AND DON'TS

- When visiting someone at home a small gift expressing your gratitude is not obligatory but would be appreciated. Value is less important than appearance, so some attractive little object, perhaps from your home country, would be appropriate, neatly and colorfully wrapped. However, don't use white paper, as white is associated with death and mourning. A box of chocolates, flowers, and fruit, presented nicely, are also appropriate. The gift will not be opened in front of you.

- Cambodians remove their shoes when entering a house, guesthouse, and some restaurants, and especially a temple, as a sign of respect.

- Be sure to remember where you leave your shoes when you are visiting a temple or any other place where many people are visiting. It can be frustrating to forget where you left them, and even more frustrating to find that someone else has mistakenly taken them for their own.

- Remove your hat. Cambodians wear hats for protection from the sun and rain and regard them as items for outdoor wear only. To wear one inside can be seen as disrespectful.

- A guest is always offered a drink of water, tea, or fruit juice. Sometimes food may be offered. It is polite to accept, even if you only take a sip or a bite. Cambodians love everything about food and a surefire way to please your host is to compliment their food and hospitality by saying "*Chhang nas*" which means "very tasty."

- In some houses you may be offered a chair, but in others, there may be mats to sit on. If that is the case, sit with your legs folded together, with your feet behind you, to one side. Don't sit with your feet straight out, with the soles of your feet facing those in front of you, and don't sit with your legs either apart or crossed.

- Never touch or pat an adult or older child on the head, which is regarded as an insult. If you need to touch a person's head—if removing something entangled in the hair or treating a wound, for instance—ask permission first.
- When passing things to other people, use the right hand or both hands, never the left, which is considered unclean. Never use your left hand for eating. The same is true for gift-giving.
- Never beckon with an upraised finger or upraised palm, which have suggestive connotations. Instead, motion with your right hand, palm down.
- When eating with chopsticks never leave the chopsticks in the bowl with ends pointing upward as they resemble the incense sticks burned for the dead. Instead, place them at the side of your plate or bowl.
- Toothpicks are usually provided at the table. When using one, it's polite to cover your mouth with the other hand.
- If you stay in the country and establish a close friendship, you may become regarded as one of the family. Should this happen, you may find yourself regarded as an honorary "uncle" or "aunt" and accepting certain obligations. In particular, you may feel obliged to take on some supportive role, particularly for a younger member of the family, perhaps assisting in education or access to employment.

CHAPTER FIVE

AT HOME

HOUSING

Housing varies enormously, from the palaces of the royal family to the humblest wooden rural dwellings—many of which are built on stilts to protect against flooding. High-ranking members of the government and the bureaucracy often occupy the gracious houses built under the French, as do many of the rich and successful in business and commerce. In the newer urban and suburban areas are spacious houses and apartments for the well-off middle and professional classes. A lot of the more modern apartments are in contemporary high-rise buildings, with features such as infinity pools, rooftop gardens, and state-of-the-art gymnasiums.

The divide between the rich and the poor is stark, with 10 million Cambodians lacking adequate housing and one in five people in urban areas living in a slum. In 2014, Cambodia adopted a National Housing Policy to promote housing development and it was predicted that

Urban housing in Phnom Penh.

an estimated 800,000 homes would be needed to meet the demand of an expected national population of 19 million by 2030. It has taken several years but the goal of affordable housing is coming closer, with five affordable housing development projects underway in 2022.

Since the influx of Chinese in 2018, the housing situation has changed dramatically in Cambodia. Poorer Cambodians with no official title deeds or property rights have lost their homes and land to foreign investors who buy the land in order to develop high-rise buildings and expensive resorts. Despite the economic impact of the pandemic, Chinese foreign direct investment hit over US $2 billion in 2021—an increase of 67 percent since 2020. Sihanoukville, in the south of Cambodia, is the hub of this investment, with millions of dollars

A stilt house on the Tonle Sap Lake.

having been funneled into altering the once idyllic coastline into a construction site of skyscrapers and fancy apartment blocks. Inevitably, this has led to the eviction of many locals and prompted the need for more affordable housing.

A feature of central urban, suburban, and town center areas is the rows of shop-houses. The shops, shuttered at night, are usually piled with goods and the owners and their families—often their extended families—live upstairs.

In rural areas there are similar shop-houses, which may be built of wood rather than concrete, again housing an extended family. On the waterways, there are moored houseboats and wooden stilted houses rising from the water and mud, and even whole floating villages, as on the Tonle Sap Lake.

DAILY LIFE AND ROUTINE

Cambodians generally rise early to enjoy the cool of the morning, and often rest during the heat of the early afternoon. When work finishes in the late afternoon, they make full use of the cool evenings and walk to visit friends or eat at local restaurants and stalls. Cambodians' lives revolve around eating—"*nam bai?*," or "have you eaten?" is commonly heard—and no matter where you go you will most likely see Cambodians sitting on plastic chairs enjoying a plate of rice and fish or chicken feet, or sour mango with chili salt.

The Working Day

Given the relaxed approach to timekeeping, it's advisable to check ahead, if possible. Government offices tend to open around 7:30 a.m. They mostly close for siesta at about 11:30 a.m., then open again from about 2:30 p.m. until 5:00 p.m. However, there will generally be few people in their offices early, and few after 4:00 p.m. Business hours for larger firms are 8:00 a.m. to 12 noon and 2:00 p.m. to 5:30 p.m. Banking hours may vary slightly according to the individual bank, but most are open from 8:30 a.m. to 3:30 p.m. on weekdays and Saturday mornings.

Museums and tourist attractions are generally open seven days a week including the lunch hour.

Local restaurants are generally open from 6:30 a.m. to 9:00 p.m., dependent on location. International restaurants stay open a little later. Most bars that serve food are open all day; others open only in the evenings. Nightclubs are to be found in Phnom Penh, Siem Reap, and the larger towns and tourist areas.

Local markets are open seven days a week, usually from 6:30 a.m. to 5:30 p.m., but it is best to get there early if you want the best produce.

SHOPPING

In recent years the range of shops and goods available has greatly improved, especially in Phnom Penh and Siem Reap. In Phnom Penh alone there are now many shopping malls, such as Aeon 1 and 2, which also house water parks, a cinema, and a craft brewery. Whether you're a long-term visitor setting up a home, or a short-term traveler, most of what you need can be found in the supermarkets, including all your food and domestic requirements. You will also find many imported products, though at a high price. The smaller family-run general stores carry a wide range of goods, and there are specialty outlets for electrical and photographic equipment, clothing, furniture, and personal and household needs. In the older shopping areas, with their traditional shop-houses, a similar supply of goods and services can be found.

Bakeries, producing a wide range of bread and cakes, are a legacy of French colonialism. Croissants and baguettes are surprisingly easy to find and are generally very high quality.

There are markets, both open and covered, which carry a wide range of goods and produce. Bear in mind

The food market at Phsar Chas, Siem Reap.

that Cambodia's textile industry has expanded greatly, and designer products can slip into the local markets and be bought cheaply. However, designer labels sometimes appear on inferior products and there are a lot of fake designer products on sale—especially in the markets— though these are usually easy to spot.

The shopping areas and markets all have restaurants, cafés, and food and drink stalls full of variety and are a great opportunity for a rest while people-watching.

Bargaining
Be prepared for some gentle bargaining in the tourist areas and local markets, but not in supermarkets

or shopping malls. Cambodians are not aggressive bargainers, but it is acceptable to try to settle on a lower price than first suggested. Merely showing a disinclination to buy may encourage a lower sale price. As a foreigner, expect the original price to be higher than a local would pay. Consider that as a visitor or expat, you are likely to be incomparably financially better off than the vendor and that a small premium will not greatly affect you. If you frequent particular shops and markets, you may also find that you will get a better price once shopkeepers and vendors recognize you as a regular customer.

THE FAMILY

The nuclear family—husband, wife, and unmarried children—is the main unit within the family structure. Emotional ties are strong and are reinforced by mutual support such as aid in times of trouble; economic cooperation in the sharing of labor, produce, and income; and the sharing of religious and ceremonial obligations and duties. In the cities, the broader family—embracing grandparents, uncles, aunts, cousins, nieces, and nephews—may also form part of the household. In rural areas, the extended family, often living together or within easy reach, is an important element of village life. Families work together as a unit to help each other and their neighbors in labor-intensive tasks such as house building and other work associated with maintaining

the village infrastructure—buildings, paths, drains, and irrigation, for example. In the towns and cities, as in the villages, the family participates in the religious life of the temple. These shared responsibilities, obligations, and services provide cohesion within both the family and the broader community.

Typically the husband is the head of the family, but the wife has considerable authority in her role as controller of the family and household budget. She also takes on the principal ethical and religious role in bringing up the children. In rural areas, there is an obvious division of labor, with the men performing the harder physical labor, such as plowing and harrowing the rice fields, caring for the cattle, buying and selling livestock, and repairing and maintaining the structure of the house. Women are mainly involved in planting, reaping, and winnowing the rice crop, tending gardens, weaving, and, as mentioned, handling the household finances. Men and women work together in the rice fields as the need arises.

Children

Even though Cambodia is growing economically, the situation for many children is still a cause for concern. While most children are shown affection and considerable freedom, many others live in poverty, or are subject to exploitation. The poorer children tend to be in the rural areas, where hospitals are few and far between, and rarely offer pediatric services. Disease and malnutrition, according to charity Humanium, are big causes of death among children as they simply don't have enough money, clean water, or the ability to access the facilities they need. AIDS, though still an issue, is less prevalent than in the past. In 2020, UNAIDS reported that 75,000 adults and children in Cambodia were living with HIV, with 1,200 deaths from AIDS. Charities, NGOs, and education have contributed to a 24 percent drop in cases since 2010. Prevention of mother-to-child transmission (PMTCT) programs offer a range of services for women of reproductive age living with or at risk of HIV to maintain their health and stop their infants from acquiring HIV. In 2020, 86 percent of pregnant women received ARV (antiretroviral therapy).

From the age of five or six, children may be expected to look after their younger siblings, and most children have started school by this age. By the time they enter school, children have learned to respect their elders and to play a role in family life: the girls will help their mother with her tasks and the boys will work with their fathers in the fields and with livestock in the country, or in their family business or with other activities in urban areas. Class differences are a factor, with the better-off children having a more privileged existence. Nevertheless, the overall experience of children's upbringing emphasizes socialization, obedience, and respect for elders and Buddhist monks. Even traditional children's games emphasize cooperation, skill, and social participation rather than winning or losing.

If you are visiting Cambodia with your family, you will find everything you need for babies and children in all the bigger cities and increasingly also in the large towns. While some people may believe that it is bad luck to buy things for a forthcoming baby, in Cambodia, even choosing the name of your unborn child is considered to be tempting fate. Many Cambodians rely on hand-me-downs from siblings or older children, but if new items are required there are lots of shops catering for prams, clothes, breastfeeding pumps, bottles, etc. Formula can even be bought online from sites such as Alibaba, Babycare, and others.

It is common for foreign children to become the center of attention among Cambodians. Parents should try to explain to them the social attitudes of their new Cambodian friends. For example, by learning how to pay respect to elders and monks they meet, their own experience will be more enjoyable.

EDUCATION

Education in Cambodia basically ceased under the Khmer Rouge. Educated and qualified people, including teachers and monks, were targeted and killed or sent to labor camps where many died. By the end of the Khmer Rouge period, over 75 percent of all educators had died or had fled the country. Beginning in 1979, the PRK government, hampered by continuing civil strife, began to revive the education system, and now offers education from preschool through to college. The main challenges faced by Cambodia's education system today include poorly educated, poorly trained, and poorly paid teachers, large class sizes, and outdated teaching methods, with great variation across the country.

Many expats who arrive looking for work in Cambodia take on teaching roles that encompass a range of subjects and ages, even if they have no qualifications. While this means that the quality of teaching in Cambodia can vary considerably, and that schoolchildren may experience a higher turnover of teachers than is ideal, it does provide an important and otherwise unfilled need for teachers who can also expose Cambodian children to Western teaching methods and help them improve their English language skills. Generally, the more highly regarded schools require a TEFOL/TESOL Certificate, a degree, and if possible, a PGCE qualification. TEFL/TESOL courses can be completed online for a fee.

The constitution prescribes free compulsory education, but its delivery is not monitored particularly closely and corruption, poverty, and family dependence on child labor, especially in rural areas, has resulted in uneven provision and attendance. Enrollment has improved in recent years; according to UNICEF, the number of children enrolled in preschool programs more than doubled from 2007 to 2020, and the number of children enrolled in primary education increased from 82 percent in 1997 to over 97 percent by 2018.

Traditionally, Cambodian education (literature, religion, and skills), took place in wats and was offered exclusively to boys. Since reform in 1996, there is now twelve years of schooling available to both boys and girls—six years for primary education (grade 1 to 6) and six years for secondary general education (grade 7 to 12). Secondary education consists of three years each for lower secondary education (grade 7 to 9) and upper secondary education (grade 10 to 12).

Currently, more than 10 percent of children do not attend school at all and nearly 20 percent of girls don't continue to high school. At upper level, the shortage of qualified teachers and adequate places in classes has led to corruption, with parents paying bribes to examiners and obtaining college places. Nevertheless, progress is being made toward improving the provision and standard of government education.

For those who can afford it, there is access to private education and institutions overseas. Chinese schools are increasingly popular in major cities, where wealthier parents encourage their children to learn Mandarin, while others send their children abroad for education.

More and more international schools are opening in Phnom Penh, Siem Reap, Kampot, Kep, Battambang, and other towns. The school day usually starts at around 8:00 a.m. with a two-hour break for lunch—usually from 11:00 a.m. to 1:00 p.m. The day ends between 3:30 p.m. and 5:00 p.m., depending on the school. In most international schools, instruction is usually split between English and Khmer, and children who have not signed up for Khmer lessons often take the afternoon off. If you're moving to Cambodia with your family, your employers and local expat groups will be able to advise you on nearby schools.

INVITATIONS HOME

In the past, entertaining formally at home was rare, though this is changing, particularly among the middle class and those who are more affluent. If you are invited to dinner at someone's home, you'll find it to be both a formal and a family affair. Elders to children will be present, and you will be an honored guest. Your host will probably be able to converse in English, but others present may not. If the hosts are not fluent in English, they may invite someone who can translate. As previously mentioned, though not obligatory, it's a good idea to bring a small gift for the host, which should be wrapped in colored paper or nicely presented. Pastries, chocolates, fruit, and flowers are all good options. Any gift should be presented with the right hand or with both hands, but never with the left hand.

Many Cambodians still eat seated on the floor, sitting in the lotus position or with legs to one side; sometimes they sit on low benches or chairs. Urban and middle-class families commonly use tables and chairs, especially for entertaining. The traditional welcoming drink is a cup of hot tea, after which food is served. The food may arrive in communal dishes, from which each diner helps themselves to their own plate or bowl.

The courses will usually be meat, fish, and vegetables in a variety of styles and served in no particular order. Your host or the person seated next to you may offer you special delicacies, which you should accept and eat, even if only a little. During the meal, there will be tea or water to drink. Cans of beer and rice wine may also be offered, although it's more often just the men drinking. Eating utensils will be either chopsticks or a spoon and fork, the fork held in the left hand and the spoon in the right. Food is eaten from the spoon, the fork is used only to push it onto the spoon. It is considered rude to put a fork in your mouth. As the left hand is unclean, it is important not to let it touch the food.

TABLE MANNERS

Whether you are being hosted at someone's home or at a restaurant by friends or colleagues, here are the main points of etiquette to be aware of:

- Wait to be told where to sit as the most senior person is usually seated first.

- Don't start eating until the most senior person has started.
- If the host chooses some food and puts it on your plate, you should eat it (or at least some of it!).
- Don't put a spoon that has been in your mouth into plates of communal food.
- Leave a little food in your bowl or on your plate to show that you've finished eating and are no longer hungry.
- When eating with chopsticks, never leave them in the bowl with the ends pointing upward as it resembles the incense sticks that are burned for the dead. Instead, lay them flat at the side of your plate or bowl.

ENTERTAINING

If you want to host your Cambodian friends, a dinner at home should proceed more or less in the way described above, perhaps with some minor Western-style variations to add interest for your guests. Find out ahead of time whether any of your guests are vegetarian or have any other dietary requirements.

Bear in mind that while many Cambodians working with expats are fluent in English, their spouses and friends may not be, and so conversation can be limited— but with a carefully devised seating plan, whether you are entertaining them at home or in a restaurant, embarrassment can be avoided.

Welcome your Cambodian friends with tea and a

selection of drinks. These should be accompanied by nuts and local nibbles offered on small plates. Remember that food must not be touched with the left hand, so the use of cocktail sticks and little plates will enable guests to pick up the snacks and eat them easily.

The meal itself could be served buffet-style, in which case invite the most prominent person present to go first and explain the contents of the dishes. If you are serving Western food at the table, do so as a Cambodian host would, describing what is in each dish as it arrives, and making sure that rice and spiced sauces are available.

After the meal, tea and coffee may be served. Cambodians regard coffee as ending both the meal and the evening, and will shortly after begin to depart, usually waiting for the first move by the most prominent guest.

With that said, attitudes and behaviors are changing, and often relations between Cambodians and their expat friends are less formal today than in the past. In general, many Cambodians who have lived, worked, or studied overseas have returned with more relaxed social attitudes.

HELP AT HOME

If you are working in Cambodia, you might be provided with accommodation, or have it found for you by your employer. In that case, it is usual to acquire some help at home, depending on the size of your accommodation and on your lifestyle. Domestic help for cleaning, laundry, and other chores is popular, and if you have a house with a garden, you may have a gardener. Many families also employ someone to help look after the children. Cambodians working for expatriates expect to have a particular job; for example, a man might be a gardener or a driver, but not both.

It's a good idea to get advice from other expats or colleagues before hiring. They will have been through the experience and will probably be able to suggest suitable candidates. Seek testimonials, and when you interview candidates have with you a person with some experience and some knowledge of the language.

Employees should be clear on what is expected of them and should be treated with respect. They will understand their role and will respond more willingly to clear direction and guidance than to direct orders. If a mistake is made, it is more in keeping with Cambodian behavior to show them what you want rather than to be angry, impatient, or critical. Nevertheless, the employer/employee relationship is a personal one, and different individuals will develop different relationships with their staff. Treat them fairly and with consideration while making clear your expectations.

When employing someone you are creating a personal relationship, not only with the individual but also with his or her family. You will be taking on some responsibility for that family and may be expected to employ another family member if you need more help or to help another family member to find employment with another expatriate. You may also be expected to help if a member of the family needs medical assistance.

CHAPTER SIX

TIME OUT

Cambodia has one of the highest numbers of public holidays anywhere in the world, so there are plenty of occasions to let your hair down. Births, weddings, and funerals too are opportunities for a big party and usually involve feasting, drinking, singing, and dancing. Big tents that sometimes take up entire streets are erected for momentous family occasions, with loud music and singing from the early morning until late at night. These are never reserved affairs and Cambodians tend to invite as many people as possible.

In their free time, Cambodians enjoy going out with family or groups of friends, often dining out together in the cool of the evening. Cafés and restaurants are full, and some restaurants have live music, which, with traditional dance, is returning to Cambodia after its suppression by the Khmer Rouge. Sports are also popular, particularly those that rely on skill, agility, and a minimum of equipment.

Musicians play traditional instruments that make up the *pinpeat* ensemble, including the circular *kong thom* gongs and *roneat ek* xylophone.

TRADITIONAL CULTURE

As part of their effort to destroy all reminders of the past, the Khmer Rouge targeted Cambodia's traditional arts. Angkor was spared as a symbol of Khmer glory, but all other artistic forms of expression were attacked. Statues, artifacts, and musical instruments were smashed, books were burned, including the contents of the National Library in Phnom Penh, and artists, writers, sculptors, musicians, and anyone associated with the arts were killed or sent into forced labor.

One of the most savage acts was the execution of all but a few of the country's classical dancers, and it has taken many years to revive that tradition. The Royal University of Fine Arts only re-established the royal ballet in 1994.

More than one thousand years old, Khmer classical dance is believed to be a
bridge of communication between the spiritual and physical realms.

Battambang, Cambodia's second-largest city, was the hub of Cambodian arts and culture for hundreds of years before it was destroyed by the Khmer Rouge in the 1970s. It is now making its mark once again for a new generation of young artists and is at the cutting edge of Cambodia's new art scene, boasting more artists per capital than any other city in Cambodia.

In Siem Reap, aside from the wonders of Angkor Wat, the art scene is vibrant and diverse with many artists preserving traditional methods, while up-and-coming artists excel with a contemporary approach.

Phnom Penh is rebuilding its artistic spirit through a group of contemporary young artists and galleries. After years of revival, where artists tended to draw on the Khmer Rouge period to create raw, heartbreaking works, times are changing and young artists in the capital are starting to look to the future and focus on optimism and change.

Khmer classical dance was associated with the royal court and is similar to the classical dance of India and Thailand. The dances are stately, and the costumes elaborate and colorful. Great importance is placed on the movement of the hands. Many bas-reliefs portraying female dancers can be found at the temples of Angkor.

Traditional music, too, has been revived. It is played on traditional instruments such as a three-stringed fiddle, a single-stringed bowed instrument, wind instruments, gongs, xylophones, and drums. These instruments are also played at weddings.

MUSIC

Cambodia has its own popular music scene, and you will hear its music and performers on Cambodian radio and television and live in the larger restaurants and bars. There are numerous local bands and DJ acts in Cambodia's cities and on the islands where live music is more popular and people dance until sunrise—a far cry from the restraints of the twentieth century. One example of contemporary Khmer music is The Kampot Playboys, a fusion Khmer-Western band that has played shows in Australia and Singapore as well as all over Cambodia. The combination of traditional Khmer and modern instruments makes for an exciting and unusual listening experience.

Legendary "golden era" singers Ros Serey Sothea (left) and Sinn Sisamouth.

During the Vietnam War, young Cambodians were exposed to American and British rock 'n' roll, which led to a new wave of Khmer musical pioneers who merged traditional Cambodian singing and melodies with the folk and rock music they encountered from abroad. The years 1960 to 1975 are internationally regarded as the "golden era" of Cambodian pop music, which saw the rise of American-influenced star performers like Ros Serey Sothea and Sinn Sisamouth. The genre and the cultural scene that grew up around it was brought to a bloody end by the Pol Pot regime, who murdered many of Cambodia's artists whom it saw as spreading foreign influence. In more recent decades there has been something of a revival of Khmer rock by local and international bands such as Dengue Fever and The Cambodian Space Project.

WATS AND PAGODAS

The great reverence held for Buddhism in Cambodia is equally extended to the temples (pagodas) and monasteries (wats) that make up its sacred and communal spaces, as well as to the monks (*prasang*) who make up the religious order, or *sangha*.

- When visiting a wat or pagoda, dress modestly, with arms and legs covered.
- Uncover your head. (This applies to women and men.)
- Remove your shoes before entering the temple sanctuary.

- Speak quietly, and in general, be restrained and respectful in your behavior. If in doubt, observe the behavior of the Cambodian worshipers around you.
- If you sit down in front of a statue of the Buddha, sit with your feet to the side, and not in the lotus position.
- Bow slightly in the presence of elderly or senior monks.
- If you are addressing a monk who is seated, be sure to sit down before addressing him; addressing a seated monk while standing is offensive.
- Women should take care to not make any physical contact with monks; not even a monk's mother is supposed to touch her son. If a woman wants to hand something to a monk, she should only put the object within his reach.
- Don't point your finger or the soles of your feet toward either a statue of the Buddha or a monk.
- Make a small contribution to the donation box; this will be appreciated by the monks and the worshipers.

SPORTS, GAMES, AND CLUBS

Cambodians engage in sports that are traditional also in other parts of Southeast Asia. Among these are kickboxing and cockfighting. Popular among young men, and requiring skill and agility, is *tapak takraw*, in which teams of four or five kick a rattan ball across a high net. Only the feet may be used, and the game requires great agility. *Sey paen* (shuttlecock kicking) is a game for all ages and is played in the open space or when there is a celebration at pagodas. It has been the most popular folk traditional game for men of all ages since ancient times and is most commonly played in open spaces in the late afternoon or pagodas during Khmer New Year and other festivals. Ball games introduced from outside, like soccer, volleyball, and basketball, are popular because they need the minimum of equipment, can be played in a relatively confined space, and demand skill and agility rather than brute strength. An annual event is the boat racing during the festival of Bom Om Tuk in early November, marking both the victory of Jayavarman (later Jayavarman VII) over the Chams and the annual reversal of the waters of the Tonle Sap. Rowing teams from across Cambodia compete, racing in traditional boats.

Before the Khmer Rouge regime, Cambodia's participation in international sports and athletics was being considered. However, facilities such as the Olympic Stadium and the National Sports Complex in Phnom Penh suffered damage and neglect under the Khmer Rouge. Now restored, they provide facilities for soccer, tennis, badminton, swimming, and other activities. The good hotels and modern apartment blocks have gyms and swimming pools, and if you are living in Cambodia you will likely have access to public facilities and private clubs through your business or social contacts. Golfers are catered for at the Royal Golf Club and the Cambodia Golf and Country Club.

Those who enjoy keeping fit and socializing should

look up the Hash House Harriers, an informal walking and running club that meets every Sunday. Mostly expats, the participants follow a trail laid earlier by two "hares" and have checks enabling the back runners to catch up while the front runners search for the next part of the trail. The run ends with refreshments, mainly beer, and is a good way to meet other expats as well as locals.

FOOD AND DRINK

Khmer cuisine is similar to Thai, but uses fewer spices. Cooked food is safe to eat though raw food should be avoided until your stomach has acclimatized. Rice is the staple food and in Khmer *nam bai* ("to eat rice") means, simply, eating. Aside from rice, fish and soup are popular staples. A fermented fish paste known as *prahoc* is a common and distinctive ingredient of many dishes. A particular specialty is *trey ahng*, which is grilled freshwater fish, wrapped in lettuce or spinach, and served with a fish sauce made with ground peanuts. Salad dishes are flavored with coriander, mint, and lemongrass. Popular and cheap dishes similar to those in neighboring countries include *bobor*, which is a rice porridge eaten at any time of day, often with fresh fish and ginger; and *kyteow*, which is a noodle soup with a mixture of ingredients and makes for a spicy and satisfying meal. *Samlor* (soup) is also popular, and among the favorites are *samlor machou banle* (hot and sour fish soup with pineapple and spices), *samlor chapek* (pork soup flavored with ginger), *samlor ktis* (fish soup with ginger and pineapple), and *samlor machou bawng kawng* (a prawn soup similar to the Thai tom yum). Other delicacies include frog, turtle, fried crickets, and tarantula.

The French have left a legacy of freshly baked bread, so croissants with coffee are available. Favorite local desserts are sticky rice cakes, sticky mango with rice and coconut milk, and jackfruit pudding. Local fruits include bananas, rambutans, pineapples, mangoes, mangosteens, and jackfruit. The strong-smelling Durian, a fruit for connoisseurs, is widely available though it should be

Clockwise from top left: Beef *lak lok;* stir fried squid with Kampot pepper; stir fried crab; *Num kachay,* fried rice flour and chive cakes.

eaten with caution—it is banned in many public places and anyone found eating it may be fined up to US $1,000!

Drinks

Tap water is cleaner than in many other places in Asia but is still regarded as unsafe to drink. Ice is generally produced from treated water, but it is still a good idea to avoid ice in drinks unless you can be sure of the source. When buying bottled water, check that the cap is secure as street sellers have been known to refill empty bottles with tap water. Otherwise, bottled soft drinks and juices are widely available, as are tea and coffee, where the water has been boiled. Tea—either hot or iced and served without milk or sugar—accompanies just about every meal.

Fruit smoothies, called *tikalok*, are popular, and in rural areas, sugarcane juice is a traditional thirst quencher. Fermented, it becomes an alcoholic beverage. You will also find ice-cold coconuts at almost every food stall.

Beer is a popular drink, and there are many local and foreign brands available, the main three being Angkor, Cambodia, and Anchor. Craft beer is becoming increasingly popular in the bigger cities, with microbreweries, such as Himarari Brewery, popping up in Phnom Penh and Siem Reap. For those who enjoy alcohol, there are fancy cocktail bars, themed bars, and rooftop bars to be found in the cities that are popular among both wealthier locals and expats alike, such as around Bassac Lane in Phnom Penh. Wines from Australia and Europe are relatively cheap, as are both local and imported spirits. However, beware of locally produced rice wine and whisky. Not only are they very strong, but there have been many instances where the production process has not been adequately supervised and mass poisoning has occurred, with sometimes fatal consequences.

EATING OUT

If you are in the country for some time, your introduction to the local restaurant and street-food scene will almost certainly be through Cambodian friends or expats who have acquired local knowledge. If you are on a short visit and staying in a hotel, ask the front desk where to eat and drink nearby. If you are feeling adventurous, simply look out for an eatery with a crowd of people—the food will very likely be good.

In Cambodia's cities, a variety of cuisines can be found—Khmer, Chinese, Thai, Vietnamese, Japanese, French, American, Italian, Indian, and Bangladeshi. Food can be enjoyed anywhere from street stalls and small, family-run businesses to upscale international-style restaurants in converted colonial villas or large hotels. Even in rural areas, there will be a café, bar, or street stall where tasty food is served and the locals eat and drink. For good food and good value, it's hard to beat the street stalls and small street-side cafés. For more formal indoor or terrace venues you will, of course, pay more, and international restaurants that usually impose a tax and service charge are more expensive again.

Women prepare lunch at a market eatery in Siem Reap.

Even in smaller establishments, menus may be bilingual, the second language usually being English, though the English version may still need deciphering. If there is no English and you don't know the Khmer word, just point to the items on display to order your choice. For those reluctant to try the local cuisine, Western-style food can be found, especially in the main tourist areas.

NIGHTLIFE

There is a stark divide in the sorts of partying that takes place in Cambodia, between the karaoke scene that

TIPPING

In most restaurants and bars, a small tip or a request to "keep the change" will be welcomed, though it is not expected. The more expensive hotels and restaurants usually impose a 10 percent service charge. Drivers and guides should receive a small tip. If you are staying at a hotel for any length of time, leave a tip for the people who clean the room. Tipping is not generally expected elsewhere.

Cambodians love and the clubbing scene more popular with expats and tourists. Wherever you are in Cambodia, a KTV (karaoke television) is never far away, and it doesn't matter how well you can sing, all are welcome and encouraged to take part. Meanwhile, there is no shortage of late-night bars and clubs in Phnom Penh, Siem Reap, Sihanoukville, and just about every other tourist area. Most expat and tourist-heavy towns and islands have regular events and late-night parties. Pub Street in Siem Reap is lined with bars and is a popular location for travelers to drink, dance, and be merry, while the Basaac Lane area in Phnom Penh offers more sophisticated and trendy bars and eateries, with nearby clubs providing opportunities to carry on partying until the early hours. Traditionally, Cambodian women avoided drinking alcohol, and only recently have single Cambodian women begun going out to bars. The girls that work in the bars and clubs are usually from poorer backgrounds, many of them from rural areas.

SHOPPING FOR PLEASURE

If you are looking for attractive mementos of your stay, there is a wide choice in Phnom Penh and Siem Reap, ranging from souvenirs aimed at tourists, to high-quality items including old and new objects, such as antiques, textiles, old coins or swords, silver, paintings, sculptures, wood carvings, jewelry, and more. There are upscale shops that cater to the affluent collector or tourist, and numerous smaller establishments and market stalls.

Newer shopping malls such as Aeon 1 and 2 in Phnom Penh offer a more modern shopping experience, with big-brand shops and food outlets, cinemas, water parks, and lots of entertainment for children. Being air-conditioned, malls also offer people respite from the heat of the day and so are popular places for people to spend time even if they aren't necessarily there to buy anything.

Bargaining

Remember that Cambodians appreciate some bargaining, but not the ferocious attempts to knock down prices that are the custom in some cultures. An apparent reluctance to buy will usually produce a lower offer, often from an inflated stated price, even in the best shops. However, in the markets and smaller shops, the asking price will not usually be overinflated and good-natured bargaining will usually produce a quick result. Cambodians are not wealthy, and the difference in the asking price and a fair price is of less consequence to you than to them. If you are living or working in the country, take some time to establish the value of particular items, consulting with both expat and Cambodian friends as to what constitutes a fair price.

Antiques

The years of conflict led to the destruction and loss of many genuine antique artifacts in Cambodia. While some were spared, the genuine article is more likely to be found in a reputable antique shop than on a market stall. Cambodian craftsmen are skilled at reproducing copies of antique objects and, as in other parts of the world, the more unscrupulous have mastered the techniques for "aging" items so that they appear genuine. Inevitably fakes are passed off as antiques, usually as Angkorian or Chinese pieces, and if the deal seems too good to be true, it probably is. If you are tempted to buy something of which you are unsure of the provenance, seek advice. Nevertheless, there are some interesting and beautiful objects available. If you see something that you can acquire for an acceptable price, it's up to you whether you like it enough to buy it, regardless of provenance.

Paintings

These range from often poor-quality pictures with an
Angkorian theme to more exciting contemporary works
that may be found in the art shops of Phnom Penh
and Siem Reap, and in galleries such as the Pi-Pet-Pi
Gallery in Phnom Penh. If you are spending some time
in Cambodia, you will have opportunities to get into the
local art scene and purchase new and fresh works by local
artists, which are produced in a wide range of techniques
and styles.

Sculpture

Sculpture is one of the most prominent art forms of
Angkor, so it is not surprising that skilled stone carvers
flourish in Cambodia today, producing replicas of ancient
works for the tourist market. Alongside them are those
who produce original work on more contemporary
themes. You may not be able to carry home a large piece
of sculpture, but there are smaller pieces that make
attractive souvenirs. Remember that it is illegal to take a
genuine Angkorian stone sculpture out of the country.

Textiles

Textiles are ideal souvenirs in that they can be easily
packed. Cambodia is particularly noted for its silk, much
of it handwoven and dyed using natural dyes. The best
silk comes from the provinces of Kampong Cham and
Takeo and can be bought from Artisans d'Angkor, which
is based in Siem Reap and has branches in Phnom Penh,
including at Psar Tuol Tom Pong and the international

airports. High-quality silk is also produced at Stung Treng and Joom Noon in Theng Meanchey province. Silk is also imported from China and Vietnam, so look for the genuine Cambodian article. Silk scarves (*krama*) are nice gifts to take home.

Wood Carving

This is another popular and highly skilled craft. Subjects include images of Buddha, carvings of Angkorian statues, betel nut boxes—that is, finely carved boxes for carrying the betel nut and the instruments for preparing it—inlaid jewelry boxes, carved animal figures, and elaborately decorated wheels used in weaving. Such items can be found in shops and markets, and it is best to look around before making a decision.

Textile production at the "silk island" of Koh Dach, near Phnom Penh.

An artist carving at the Artisans Angkor workshop in Siem Reap.

Silver

Cambodian silver is renowned for its beauty and the
fine detail of its craftsmanship. However, silver needs
an alloy to give it strength, and the silver content of
pieces for sale ranges from insignificant to almost pure
silver. It can be difficult to tell the difference and be sure
of what you are buying. A reputable shop should tell
you the percentage of silver to alloy in its pieces while
market sellers may not.

Furniture

It is possible to buy beautifully handcrafted furniture.
If you will be a resident for some time you may want
to buy pieces to take home when your stay is over.
Traditional and very heavy Khmer furniture with
intricate carving and mahogany wood is highly

sought after by locals, and due to the extortionate price tag, pieces are considered status symbols and a sign of wealth.

Clothes

Cambodia produces clothing for several international brands. Look in the upscale boutique-style shops, the large stores, shopping malls, clothing and textile shops in the bazaars, and the markets, especially Psar Tuol Tom Pong (see below). Beware of the many fake items, however, which are generally easy to spot due to the dubious spelling of brands.

MARKETS

The main market in Phnom Penh is the Psar Thiem, also known as the Central Market. It's housed under a huge dome with four wings and filled with all kinds of goods from gold to clothing. Stop for refreshment at one of the many food and drink stalls, and watch the world go by.

Psar Tuol Tom Pong is the best market for shopping for everything from souvenirs, crafts, silk, textiles, and antiques, both real and fake, and is very popular with tourists. It is called the Russian Market because it was popular with Russian visitors during the 1980s.

Psar O Russel and Psar Olympic in Phnom Penh, as well as Psar Chaa in Siem Reap, are large indoor markets also worth visiting.

Payment remains predominantly cash-only, with card payments available in larger shopping malls and some hotels. Though most Cambodian people have smartphones and use online banking, contactless payment is not currently widespread.

PHOTOGRAPHY

There are many beautiful photographs to be taken in Cambodia. When photographing people, it is best to show respect by asking for permission before taking their picture. This is particularly the case when it comes to monks and worshipers. Cambodians are courteous and will usually agree to have their photograph taken, if asked. Children may be delighted to have their picture taken, especially if they can see themselves on your camera screen after. And, with the rise of smartphones, you may find yourself at the receiving end of a camera lens, too!

CHAPTER SEVEN

TRAVEL, HEALTH, & SAFETY

ARRIVAL

The easiest way to enter Cambodia is to fly in to either Phnom Penh or Siem Reap, both of which service international flights including from regional hubs such as Bangkok, Kuala Lumpur, Singapore, Ho Chi Minh City, Vientiane, Hong Kong, and Guangzhou—to name just a few. The airport at Phnom Penh is 4.5 miles (7 km) from the city, and taxis are relatively cheap, particularly if you are prepared to share. Shared taxis can be quite an experience as drivers will try to cram as many passengers in as possible, and you may even end up with someone on your lap. Buses and shared taxis also ferry passengers to the Thai, Laos, and Vietnamese border crossings where you can either change to a new vehicle or continue in the same one to your destination. Night buses are notoriously dangerous and are not advised.

Passport and visa requirements for entry are straightforward. You will need a valid passport expiring no sooner than six months from your planned departure date. Tourist visas for one month are obtainable on entry and online before leaving your country of residence. These can be renewed for one month only. You will need to submit a passport-sized photo as part of the visa process. Business visas cost more but can be extended for longer periods—three, six, and twelve months. Note that the three-month business visas do not allow for multiple entry into Cambodia. Be aware also that entry and visa requirements are liable to change, as during the Covid-19 pandemic. Contact the Cambodian Embassy in your home country for current requirements.

TRAVEL WITHIN THE COUNTRY

Cambodia's infrastructure was badly damaged during the years of conflict. However, much has been repaired and upgraded, and moving around the country by air, land, and water today is largely trouble free.

By Road
In the past few years, considerable investment and international aid has been utilized to develop Cambodia's major roads and upgrade them to expressways where appropriate, as between Phnom Penh and Sihanoukville, Phnom Penh and Kampot, and from Phnom Penh to Siem Reap and Battambang. New roads are being built

A moto with pasengers in Phnom Penh.

all the time due to ongoing development and Chinese investment.

Driving can be treacherous as people rarely follow the rules. Drink driving is common and you should always stay alert. During the rainy season, roads can become extremely flooded and many potholes develop, which can be dangerous, especially when you cannot see how deep they are because they are filled with water.

Cars and motorcycles are available for rent. If you wish to drive yourself, you should have an international driver's license. No license is required for renting a motorcycle, however. If you are working in Cambodia or staying for any length of time and intend to drive, then a Cambodian license will be required, although most expats hire a driver.

Conditions on the road can be chaotic. Traffic in Cambodia drives on the right-hand side of the road, as in the US and continental Europe. However, this is loosely interpreted. Many Cambodians have never taken a driving test and their driving skills and knowledge of traffic rules are variable. More importantly, much of the road traffic is slow. Bicycles are used to carry not only the rider but often surprisingly large loads. At the next level is the "moto," a small motorbike that is used to its utmost capacity to carry passengers, frequently a whole family perched before and behind the driver. Motos are often converted to carry large loads by having a shelf attached behind the rider, or a trailer. They are unlicensed, yet their owners compete to perform a taxi service, picking up passengers at the curbside and weaving through the traffic to their destination—these are called motodops and are a cheap way to travel.

Taxis are plentiful, each determined to get the journey over quickly in order to pick up the next passenger. There are currently four ride-hailing apps in service in Cambodia. These are GrabTaxi, PassApp, Tada, and WeGo Taxi App. Service varies from city to city, and while Grab accepts card payment, the rest require cash.

Motorists have to get through the jumble of slower traffic and keep an eye open for faster and nippier motorcyclists who weave in and out and often cut across from one side of the road to the other. In rural areas, there are also hazards caused by animals wandering onto roadways.

A car is useful for getting around Phnom Penh and Siem Reap, and gives you the freedom to take your time at places of interest. However, it is safer and less stressful to hire a vehicle and driver. Look for recommended drivers online and ask locals or expats for the best option. If you intend to travel out of town or tour more widely, the cost is higher and you will need to pay for the driver's accommodation and food as well as your own. Gas prices are significantly higher in the countryside.

Motorcycles can also be rented in Phnom Penh and other cities and towns, but riders should be aware of the hazardous traffic conditions and make sure to wear a helmet. Traveling by motorcycle in the countryside is not recommended for the novice.

Buses

Bus travel has improved with the roads, and modern, air-conditioned coaches provide regular services between Phnom Penh and the other major cities and towns, including Siem Reap, Battambang, Takeo, Kampong Cham, and Kampot. Check online for your desired route using camboticket.com, where you can also buy tickets. Tickets are also available from hotels and street kiosks. Tickets are numbered, so there is no overcrowding. Bus travel is very affordable, and services are regular and reliable.

Minibuses also operate, but they do not keep a regular schedule and leave when they're full. If they have air-conditioning, it may not work too well. Fewer people use minibuses, but if you have the time and want to meet ordinary Cambodians, you will enjoy doing so. If you need to make a delivery to another city, minibuses will offer a good price.

Rail Travel

Cambodia has two railway lines, one from Phnom Penh to Banteay Meanchey and a second from Phnom Penh to Sihanoukville, the nation's deep-sea port. In 2021 the Ministry of Public Works and Transport began drafting a railway development strategy to revamp and extend the national network, which is seen as critical to the country's continued development. Traveling by train is a good way to see some spectacular scenery and to meet people. Fellow passengers will be curious about you, and if they have enough English, will likely want to talk to you.

Boat Travel

Cambodia has 1,900 km of navigable waterways. Express boats operate between Phnom Penh and Siem Reap, and Sihanoukville and islands such as Koh Rong and Koh Rong Sanloem. There are also slower and cheaper services. The route between Phnom Penh and Siem Reap crosses the vast expanse of the Tonle Sap, which is not particularly picturesque, but the route is popular with locals and tourists. Boat services up the Mekong depart from Kampong Cham, which is accessible by road from Phnom Penh. Traveling along the Mekong by boat is more scenic, and at Kratie you may even see freshwater dolphins. There is also an attractive river route between Siem Reap and Battambang.

Air Travel

There are several regular daily flights between Phnom Penh and Siem Reap, and flights also from Phnom Penh to other regional capitals, as well as various Chinese cities. There is also a small airport in Sihanoukville where you can catch flights to Phnom Penh, Siem Reap, three Chinese cities, Manila, Macau, Kuala Lumpur, Ho Chi Minh City, Kunming, Shanghai, and Hong Kong.

As of 2022, three further international airports were under construction—one in Phnom Penh, one in Siem Reap, and one in Koh Kong Province.

HEALTH AND MEDICAL CARE

Cambodia's health services suffered heavily under the Khmer Rouge. Despite government efforts, which are continuing to bring improvement, they are still of variable standard. Good medical facilities are available in the larger cities, but the countryside is still poorly served. If you become ill while you are outside urban areas, you should return to them for treatment. Phnom Penh has the best hospitals—The Royal Phnom Penh hospital and Calmette Hospital amongst others—but if your medical condition is very serious you may be sent to Bangkok or Ho Chi Minh.

Medical Care

If you are working in Cambodia, you will likely have access to medical care arranged by or through your employer. If you are on vacation, you should have medical insurance to cover any medical expenses you may incur, but you will need to pay upfront and in cash before you can file a claim. If you have a condition requiring special medication you should bring a sufficient supply for the duration of your time in Cambodia; however, pharmacies carry a wide range of medicines for most common ailments.

The best medical facilities are in Phnom Penh and Siem Reap. Away from those centers, local government facilities are often rather basic and you might have difficulty making yourself understood there. Therefore, if you will be traveling outside the main centers, seek advice from a good hotel or an embassy or consulate and obtain the names and locations of individual local doctors and clinics near the places you will be traveling. If you are with a group, the tour operator will have the necessary information.

Like all tropical countries, Cambodia is home to diseases and infections that are less prevalent and more easily treated in the cities. Greater caution has to be observed if traveling in rural areas. You should carry medicine and first-aid equipment and take all available preventive measures. On an organized tour, the risks will be slight and advice will be available.

The list of health risks listed below may appear daunting, but Cambodia is no less safe than any other country in the region if you stay within reasonable bounds, observe elementary hygiene, and take the necessary precautions.

Hepatitis B used to be endemic in Cambodia. There are six types of viral hepatitis with similar symptoms. These include a general lassitude and physical debilitation accompanied by fever, headaches, chills, general aches and pains, nausea, vomiting, dark urine, light-colored feces, jaundiced skin, and yellowing of the whites of the eyes. However, since the hepatitis B vaccine was added into the national immunization program in 2005, Hepatitis B rates have dramatically reduced.

Hepatitis A and E can cause acute illness, but there is a vaccine and you will eventually recover. Rest, drink plenty of fluids, eat lightly, and avoid fatty foods. Hepatitis A and E are transmitted via fecal-oral contact and are a product of unsanitary conditions. Elementary hygiene reduces risk.

Hepatitis B and D have similar symptoms to types A and E, but type B can be more severe and can lead to long-term liver damage, liver cancer, and the risk of being a long-term carrier. Both types are transmitted via blood, saliva, semen, and vaginal fluids. A vaccine is available.

Hepatitis C is transmitted only by blood-to-blood contact. At the time of writing, there is no vaccine. Type G hepatitis is not dangerous.

Malaria is spread by mosquitoes and is potentially fatal. In areas where it is endemic, mostly in the northern regions and in the jungle, take antimalarial tablets and try to avoid being bitten. Wear long-sleeved shirts and long trousers, especially in the evenings, use mosquito coils, and sleep under mosquito nets. The symptoms include fever, headache, chills and sweating, diarrhea, abdominal pains, and a general feeling of illness. Medication is available. There are various forms of malaria, so check with your health provider on the proper medication required for wherever you are traveling to.

Typhoid is transmitted via food and water and is an enteric disease caused by a type of salmonella bacteria. Early symptoms are similar to influenza, with fever, headache, loss of appetite, and a general feeling of illness. You may experience constipation or diarrhea. Fever and headache may become more severe and a red skin rash and sore throat may develop. Jaundice can be another symptom. Typhoid can be confused with malaria but with typhoid, the pulse rate is relatively slow for a person with a fever. About 10–30 percent of cases become serious and it is advisable to seek medical advice as soon as any symptoms occur.

Rabies is a fatal viral infection transmitted through the saliva of furry animals such as dogs, cats, bats, and monkeys, and is not dependent on a bite. It may pass through the saliva into a cut or scratch—made by the animal or already present. If you are licked or bitten by such an animal, clean the area promptly and thoroughly with soap and running water, and disinfectant, alcohol, or iodine, and seek immediate medical attention. A course of injections will prevent the onset of symptoms.

Japanese B Encephalitis is a mosquito-borne infection of the brain that occurs in the rural rice-growing areas. Travelers are at low risk. There is a vaccine, but take precautions against mosquito bites as outlined above in the note on malaria.

SAFETY

Don't wander off the beaten track. Unexploded ordnance—shells, mortars, rockets, bombs, and mines—is a possible hazard. From 1979 to 2019, landmine and UXO explosions had killed 19,780 people and injured 45,075 others. Cambodia has done much to eradicate the problem, but it is estimated that there are from four to six million unexploded mines still littering the countryside. All main roads have been cleared, but do not depart from them. If you are in a remote area, keep to the road or track, and seek advice before traveling. If you are living in the country, you will soon become aware of the problem and the precautions to take when traveling to places of interest. The main tourist sites are safe but keep within their boundaries. Cambodia has pledged to address all its landmine contamination by 2025.

The years of conflict have also left many firearms in circulation, though gun crime is not as common as might be expected. Nonetheless, travelers are warned to be cautious, especially at night and in rural areas. Motorcycle thefts and robberies are more likely in Phnom Penh, Siem Reap, and Sihanoukville than elsewhere. Walking and riding alone late at night is not advisable. However, as in any other country, there is little danger if sensible precautions are taken.

Tourists may be targeted by pickpockets, especially in the markets and at night, although basic precautions can reduce the likelihood. Don't leave belongings unattended, and keep money and valuables safely out of sight. A common trick is for moto riders to drive past and swipe your cell phone from your hands or pull your handbag off your shoulder. Wherever you are, be aware of your surroundings.

PLACES TO VISIT

There are many reasons to visit Cambodia. It is endowed with great natural beauty, abundant wildlife, and a rich and ancient culture. Cambodians are proud of their heritage, especially of that left of the great Khmer empire centered on Angkor. This was the one part of Cambodia's heritage that was not attacked and desecrated, the Khmer Rouge retaining it as a symbol of Khmer pride and identity. With the passing of the regime, the old arts have been revived. Linked to the commercialism that inevitably accompanies tourism is pride in their ancient past, just as there is shame for their more recent experiences under the Khmer Rouge. Significantly, they have retained the scenes of atrocity as memorials to the depths to which Cambodia sank, in the hope that such things may never happen again.

Phnom Penh

Phnom Penh, despite recent history, retains a charm based on its royal and colonial past. The French left a legacy of colonial architecture that still provides a pleasing backdrop to the busy street life, now reinforced by the redevelopment of the waterfront, which is

Phnom Penh

especially lively on Friday and Saturday nights and during festivals, and the creation of new trendy areas full of bars, eateries, and nightclubs. Phnom Penh and Sihanoukville have quite large Chinese populations, and Chinese New Year is a good time to see dragon dances in the streets and Chinese lanterns light up the sky.

As the royal capital after the move from Angkor, the city possesses many impressive wats and palaces. The Silver Pagoda is the most spectacular temple and was preserved by the Khmer Rouge as a repository of Khmer culture. Among the other wats of importance are Wat Ounalon, Wat Phnom, and Wat Moha Montrei.

Sihanoukville

Sihanoukville (Kampong Saom), the port city on the southern coast, used to be infamous for its white sandy beaches, access to unspoiled tropical islands, excellent fresh seafood, and active nightlife. However, in recent years, Sihanoukville, as one of the major cities on China's Belt and Road Initiative, has seen dramatic changes as a result of extraordinary levels of Chinese investment into the city. An influx of Chinese workers, developers, and investors settling in the city has caused a demographic shift, which has not been necessarily welcomed by all. The development of numerous construction projects has generated resentment among local people, and anger among those subjected to forced evictions to make way for new roads and buildings. As of 2020, some eighty thousand Chinese lived in Sihanoukville, accounting for 90 percent of the city's expat population. Mandarin signage adorns shop fronts and restaurants, replacing the Khmer and English of the past. The city is served by an international airport, which is undergoing a major twenty-year development program which includes a major runway extension and a new passenger terminal. Sihanoukville's port is the gateway to the islands Koh Rong Sanloem, Koh Rong, and Koh Ta Kiev, among others.

The Killing Fields of Choeung Ek
A white stupa marks the location of 125 mass graves, forty-three of which remain untouched, and is a memorial to the seventeen thousand people executed here by the Khmer Rouge between mid-1975 and December 1978. Displayed on shelves behind the stupa's glass panels are the skulls of eight thousand victims,

many of them bludgeoned to death to save bullets. This was not the only place of execution but remains as a symbol of the regime's brutality and a memorial to all those who died in similar circumstances.

Phnom Sontuk

Situated in Cambodia's northwest, this holy mountain is adorned with pagodas and statues of the Buddha. Rising high above the surrounding countryside, it is approached by a forest path with 980 steps, arriving at a colorful pagoda with many small shrines. Images of the Buddha have been carved into large sandstone boulders. Beneath the southern summit lie generations of reclining Buddhas, the oldest carved into the rock centuries ago, some of the more recent images cast in cement. The monks at the wat on the mountain are pleased to welcome tourists.

Kampong Thom, midway between Phnom Penh and Siem Reap, is worth using as a base from which to visit both Phnom Sontuk and the pre-Angkorian temples associated with the Chenla capital of Sambor Prei Kuk.

Kirirom National Park

Located at Phnom Sruoch district in the province of Kampong Speu and set in highland pine forests, this area offers good walking trails and sightings of many beautiful waterfalls. This park is also home to many endangered species of animals such as the pleated gibbon, sun bear, and tiger. Kirirom National Park is part of the Southwest Cluster Protected Areas

A temple set in the hills of Kirirom National Park.

which include Phnom Bokor, Preah Sihanouk, and Kep National Parks.

Bokor National Park

Located in the southern tip of the Elephant Mountains, this park has a cool climate. It was formerly a French colonial hill station: a road was first made in 1925 and the hill resort was established at 1,080 m. The French left in the late 1940s, and it was abandoned to the Khmer Rouge in the early 1970s. Bokor Mountain was known for its eerie, ghost-like feel, with the desolate, crumbling buildings projecting a certain spookiness lingering from its violent past. However, Bokor has undergone some dramatic changes, with Chinese investment in major building projects. Some of these have come at a cost to the natural environment. You can still visit the old, abandoned church and the king's former residence, called the Black Palace. There are waterfalls, and panoramic views of the ocean to be enjoyed from Wat Sampov Pram, as well as a hydroponic farm. The centerpiece of the resort was the grand Bokor Palace Hotel, which has been renovated in its original style and now includes a casino.

Siem Reap

Most people visiting or working in Cambodia visit Siem Reap, the gateway to the ruins of Angkor. The town itself retains much of its French colonial charm, with a pleasant riverfront, tree-lined boulevards, and busy shop-houses, with cafés and restaurants. A lot of new developments sit alongside the old, and tourism has increased prices, along with traffic. Areas in the main part of town, such as Pub Street, are less salubrious at night, with a lot of drunken activity and some petty theft. Nevertheless, its proximity to the splendors of Angkor makes it a worthwhile stop.

The Temples of Angkor

A visit to Angkor is a must for all visitors to Cambodia, which does make it somewhat of a tourist hotspot. Since the 1990s, Angkor Wat has become a major tourist destination. In 1993, there were only 7,650 visitors to the site, but by 2019 this number had reached well over 2 million. During the coronavirus pandemic Angor Wat was closed to stop the spread of the virus but reopened to travelers in late 2021.

The temples and palaces of Angkor represent the

height of classic Khmer civilization and demonstrate its wealth and power, its artistic, architectural, and engineering achievements, and the hubris that caused its eventual collapse. Glorifying its rulers and their conquests, the carved temple friezes show battles against the Thais and the Chams and the procedures of government, ritual, war, and justice. One depicts the torture chambers of Hell, and presumably those of the king, indicating that the events of recent years reflected a dark side of Khmer governance and society that had not previously been unknown. Also present are images reflecting the beauty, grace, and culture of the court, the religious contemplation of its inhabitants, the occupations of its people, and the expression of its faiths. Less immediately obvious, except in the lakes and channels still visible, is the skill of the hydraulic engineers of the time, who produced a water supply and irrigation system depending on minute differences in levels, accurately measured to enable the constant flow of the water upon which the life of this great civilization depended. A good time to visit, although often crowded, is sunrise, where you will get beautiful photographs to treasure.

Admission Passes

Visitors must obtain a pass, which can be bought via your hotel, online, or at the entrance booth on the way to Angkor Wat. This allows access to all the main temples within the Siem Reap Angkor area. Passes are available for one day, three days, or a week, and cannot be extended. A multiday pass requires a passport-size photograph, so bring one with you or be prepared to stand in line for an instant photograph. How long you obtain a pass for depends on how you choose to get around and how many of the hundreds of temples you want to see. It is possible to see quite a lot of the Angkor complex in a single day, including the obvious highlights. More days will enable you to venture to temples further out, or to take things a bit easier. Guards check the tickets at the main attractions but are not at the smaller temples. However, you will have to pay a fine if you are found in a temple complex without a pass. Be sure to check what your pass covers, as some of the remoter attractions aren't included. Passes bought after 5:00 p.m. are valid from the following day. No pass is required to visit nearby villages.

Moving Around the Site

Angkor is huge and walking from one temple to the next is inadvisable. You'll need to do plenty of walking at each of the temples and you will have to climb countless stairs. There are numerous ways of getting around to see the temples, and your choice may depend on the number traveling together, the weather, your fitness, and the time and money you have to spend. The three ways to get around Angkor are by tour van, tutkuk, or bicycle. These can all be arranged in Siem Reap, either in a hotel or at a local tour operating service. Foreigners are not allowed to ride a moto inside the complex.

THE TEMPLE COMPLEX OF ANGKOR

The following is a list of the major sites at Angkor within easy reach of Siem Reap. Once in Cambodia, you will be able to obtain a detailed map of all the sites at Angkor, and any tourist office or hotel will have further information. There are, of course, guidebooks devoted to the temples, and these pages set out to describe only the main scenes and events depicted on the walls of the most important temples. There is in most cases a sequence of images, which makes the story clear, and this is worth understanding before a first visit.

Angkor Wat

Probably built by King Suryavarman II (1112–52) both to honor Vishnu and as his own mausoleum, the temple is oriented to the west, the direction associated with Vishnu and with death. It is the largest and best preserved of the temples at Angkor and is believed to be the biggest religious site in the world. The whole complex is a replication of the Hindu universe. The central tower represents Mount Meru, rising over the lower peaks represented by the lower towers. The courtyards are the continents and the outer moat the oceans. The seven-headed naga serpent represents the rainbow bridge between man and heaven. The dimensions are such that in walking across the causeway to the main entrance and then continuing through the successive courtyards to the central tower, one metaphorically travels back in time to the creation of the universe. Each stage represents one of the four ages of classical Hindu thought. The huge scale of the structure is awesome. The moat is 190 m wide and forms a rectangle measuring 1.5 km by 1.3 km. The stone for the temple was quarried more than 50 km away and carried down the Siem Reap River on rafts before being manhandled into position. The main entrance is through a large and richly decorated porch 258 m wide on the western side. In a gate tower to the right is a large statue of Vishnu, which is still revered. From the entrance, a long, broad avenue leads to the main temple. It is lined with naga balustrades and passes between two libraries and two pools before arriving at the entrance to the central temple. This is built on three levels, which enclose a square surrounded by interlinked galleries. The Gallery of a Thousand Buddhas is one of these, but it is now greatly depleted and the remaining statues are severely damaged.

The second and third stories have towers at their corners, and from the middle rises the great central tower. The central sanctuary once housed a gold statue of Vishnu riding a *garuda*, part man, part bird, which represented the deified god-king Suryavarman II. The stairs to this upper level are extremely steep and should be climbed with great caution. Once at the summit, however, pause, relax, and absorb the amazing view and the sense of wonder this great monument evokes.

At ground level, further wonder awaits you. The vast inner wall of the cloister surrounding the lower level is covered with bas-reliefs, the great majority dating from the twelfth century, with some added in the sixteenth. Starting at the western wall, and keeping the wall to your left, you will see the following in turn.

The Battle of Kurukshetra
On the southern wall of the west gallery is depicted a scene from the Hindu epic Mahabharata. The Kauravas, coming from the left, meet the Pandavas, coming from the right. Infantry are shown on the lowest tier, with officers on elephants and chiefs on the second and third tiers. The carving is detailed and clear, and highly polished by being touched by millions of hands.

The Army of Suryavarman II
The western section of the south gallery shows the army of Suryavarman II. The king, wearing a coronet and carrying a battle-axe, is seated on an elephant; he is shaded by fifteen umbrellas and fanned by servants. Then there are officers and chiefs on horseback, among them chiefs on elephants. The Khmer soldiers wear square breastplates and carry spears. Further on is a depiction of the supporting Thai mercenary army, less well-ordered, wearing long headdresses and skirts and carrying tridents.

Heaven and Hell
The eastern half of the south gallery depicts the rewards of the thirty-seven heavens and the punishments of the thirty-two hells. On the left, the upper and middle tiers show gentlemen and ladies processing toward an

eighteen-armed Yama, judge of the dead, seated on a hill, with his assistants, Dharma and Sitragupta, below him. On the lower level is the road to hell, along which the wicked are dragged by devils. To Yama's right the tableau is divided horizontally by a line of *garuda*, the upper level depicting heaven, where the elect dwell in beautiful mansions served by servants, women, and children, while below the condemned suffer the tortures of hell.

The Churning of the Sea of Milk

The southern section of the east gallery depicts the Churning of the Sea of Milk. Beautifully executed, this relief depicts eighty-eight *asura* (demons) on the left and ninety-two *deva* (gods) to the right churning up the sea of milk to extract the elixir of immortality that both desire. The demons hold the head of the serpent and the gods the tail. At the center, the serpent is coiled around Mount Mandala, which in the tug-of-war is turned and churns up the sea. Vishnu, incarnated as a giant turtle, lends his shell as the base and pivot upon which Mount Mandala turns. Present also are Brahma, Shiva, Hanuman, the monkey god, and Lakshmi, goddess of beauty. Above, a host of *apsaras* (heavenly nymphs) sing and dance, encouraging the gods and distracting the demons.

Elephant Gate

This gate, which has no stairs leading to it, was used by the king and others of rank to mount and dismount from elephants directly from the gallery.

Vishnu Conquering the Demons
The northern section of the east gallery depicts a furious battle between Vishnu, mounted on a *garuda*, and a horde of *danava* (demons), who are getting the worst of it. Carved probably in the sixteenth century, this is inferior to the earlier reliefs.

Krishna and the Demon King
The eastern section of the north gallery depicts Vishnu incarnated as Krishna mounted on a *garuda* before a burning walled city, the residence of the demon king Bana. The *garuda* puts out the fire and Bana is captured. In the final scene, Krishna kneels before Shiva and asks that Bana's life be spared.

The Battle of the Gods and the Demons
The western section of the north gallery depicts a battle between the twenty-one gods of the Hindu pantheon and various demons. The gods are recognizable by their traditional attributes and mounts. For example, Vishnu has four arms and is mounted on a *garuda*, while Shiva rides a sacred goose.

The Battle of Lanka
The northern half of the west gallery depicts scenes from the Ramayana. In the battle of Lanka, Rama, on the shoulder of Hanuman, along with his army of monkeys battles the ten-headed Ravana, seducer of Rama's wife, Sita. Ravana rides in a chariot drawn by monsters and commands an army of giants.

Angkor Thom

Built by Angkor's greatest king, Jayavarman VII (1181–
1219), Angkor Thom replaced the previous Khmer
capital sacked by the Chams. A fortified city, it is enclosed
by a square wall 8 m high and 12 km in length, and
circled by a moat 100 m wide, said to have been inhabited
by crocodiles. The city has five monumental gates, one
in each of the northern, western, and southern walls
and two in the eastern wall. The gates are 20 m high,
decorated with stone elephant trunks and crowned with
four gigantic faces of the Bodhisattva Avalokiteshvara
facing the cardinal directions: this is a Buddhist city, not
Hindu, even though its design echoes the concept of
Mount Meru surrounded by the oceans. The temple at
its center is the Bayon, and this is a Buddhist monument.
Yet, outside the gates, the balustrades of the causeways
over the moat replicate the Churning of the Sea of Milk
with fifty-four gods to the left of the causeway and
fifty-four demons to the right. The south gate has been
restored, and being on the main road into Angkor from
Siem Reap is very busy. The east and west gates are more
peaceful and are accessible.

Bayon

At the center of Angkor Thom lies the Bayon, which as
well as replicating Mount Meru is a grand expression of
Jayavarman VII's power and majesty. In form it is a large
platform with three levels, the top level supporting fifty-
four towers bearing 216 huge faces of Avalokiteshvara,
enigmatic and smiling, representing the presence of the

The stone faces of Avalokiteshvara at Bayon Temple.

king—powerful, but benign, and always present. Oriented to the east, it is often visited in the morning, but it is magnificent at any time and best experienced in relative solitude.

The temple is on three levels. The first two levels are square and adorned with bas-reliefs. The third level is circular and has towers and faces. There is 1.2 km of bas-reliefs, the most outstanding being those on the first level. If you enter the Bayon by the eastern gate and move clockwise around the first level, the panels are in the following sequence.

The Defeat of the Chams

Of the three tiers, the lowest shows Khmer soldiers marching to battle with elephants and ox carts. The middle tier shows coffins being carried from the battlefield. The third tier depicts Jayavarman VII on horseback, shaded by parasols and with a retinue of concubines.

Worshiping the Linga
The first panel north of the southeastern corner shows
Hindus praying to a phallic symbol, the lingam. This
image may have originally been a Buddha, later
modified by a Hindu king.

Naval Battle on the Tonle Sap
The sequence contains graphic images of the naval battle
fought against the Chams, whose heads are covered,
and also scenes of everyday life and the preparation and
serving of the feast that celebrated the Khmer victory.
Note the crocodiles in the lake waiting for their victims.

Tiger Chase
The last section of the south gallery depicts a military
procession, a scene of elephants being brought in from
the mountains, and a humorous scene of Brahmans
being chased up two trees by tigers.

Conflict
A series of scenes appear to depict a civil war, beginning
with groups of people confronting each other and
escalating into a general conflict with soldiers and
elephants.

The All-Seeing King
The next panel also shows fighting. In another image, a
large fish swallows an antelope. Among the smaller fish
is a prawn under which an inscription proclaims that the
king will seek out those in hiding.

Victory
A victory parade, with the king carrying a bow.

Royal Circus
The panel at the western corner of the northern wall depicts a circus. Among the performers is a strongman holding three dwarfs, a man on his back spinning a wheel with his feet, and a group of tightrope walkers. The royal court watches from a terrace, and below is a procession of animals.

Bountiful River
Two rivers, both teeming with fish.

Battle Scenes
The rest of the north wall carries extensive battle scenes between the Chams and the Khmers. The first shows the defeat and expulsion of the Chams, the second the Cham army advancing, and the third the Chams in pursuit of fleeing Khmers. The story is continued on the northern panels of the eastern wall, where the Chams are shown sacking Angkor, the wounded king being lowered from the back of an elephant, and a wounded Khmer general being carried in a hammock suspended from a pole, while the Chams pursue the fleeing Khmers.

The final panel depicts another meeting of the two armies, the flags of the Chams being a distinctive feature.

The reliefs on the second level of the Bayon are not as spectacular as those on the first level and do not make as clear a sequence, but they are well worth viewing.

Terrace of the Leper King

The twelfth-century Terrace of the Leper King is a
7-m-high platform that takes its name from a nude but
sexless statue. The significance of this figure is unclear;
one view is that it represents a Khmer king who had
leprosy, another that it represents Yama, the god of death.
In either case, the terrace may mark the site where the
king was cremated.

The front retaining walls of the terrace are adorned
with five tiers of exquisitely carved seated apsaras, kings,
courtiers, and princesses wearing pearls. The terrace was
originally topped by a pavilion.

On the southern side of the terrace, which faces the
Terrace of Elephants, there is access to the front wall of a

Bas-relief sculpture at the Terrace of the Leper King.

terrace that was covered when the larger one was built.
The four tiers of carvings here are as fresh as when
first constructed.

Terrace of Elephants

The Terrace of Elephants is on a grand scale: 350 m long,
it was a viewing stand for the king and the base of the
great audience hall. From here the king and his court in
all their magnificence and glory would view the parades
of elephants, horses, chariots, and soldiers in the Grand
Square. The terrace has five outworks extending into the
square: three in the center and one at each end. The middle
section of the retaining wall of the terrace is decorated with
life-size *garuda* and lions. Toward each end are the parades
of elephants that give the terrace its name. Around Angkor
Thom are further buildings.

Ta Prohm

At Ta Prohm time has stood still. It is the nearest you
will get to experience the wonder and awe that gripped
the first European discoverers of Angkor as they found
its ruins in the jungle. That jungle has been cut back
and thinned to provide access, but the larger trees
remain, rising from the stones, their huge roots twisting
and curling around the stones. It is forbidden to enter
the damaged galleries for fear of accidents. However,
enough is accessible to give you some idea of what it
must have been like. The main problem is that you
are very unlikely to be left alone to enjoy any quiet
reflection on the matter.

Phnom Bakheng

A favorite site from which to view Angkor Wat at sunset, Phnom Bakheng can be crowded. This was the first of the temple mountains constructed by Yasovarman I (889–910). The temple was built in accordance with Hindu cosmology.

Prasat Pravan

This is a Hindu complex with five brick towers. Built in 921, although not by royalty, and partially restored in 1968, it is remarkable for its magnificent carvings on the inner brick walls. The central tower has two large images, one on the back wall depicting Vishnu taking the three strides with which he traversed the universe, and the other, on the right wall, of Vishnu riding a *garuda*. The northernmost tower has carvings of Vishnu's consort, Lakshmi.

Banteay Kdei and Sra Srang

Banteay Kdei is a Buddhist monastery built in the latter part of the twelfth century but never fully completed, and much of it is in ruins. It is surrounded by four concentric walls. Its four entrances are decorated with *garuda*, which hold aloft the four faces of Avalokiteshvara. Nearby and to the east of Banteay Kdei is Sra Srang (the Pool of Ablutions), a vast reservoir, constructed before the temple and decorated with naga heads. A small island in the middle once bore a wooden temple, of which only the base remains.

Ta Keo

This undecorated and unfinished temple, dedicated to Shiva, was built by Jayavarman V (968–1001). The temple mountain is crowned by a 50-m tower, which is surrounded by four lesser towers at each corner of the upper platform. Even without the decoration that it would have had if completed, it is an impressive structure and the first at Angkor that was built entirely of sandstone.

Thommanon

Dedicated to Shiva and Vishnu, this temple underwent extensive restoration in the 1960s.

Preah Khan

One of the largest complexes at Angkor, Preah Khan bears comparison with Ta Prohm, and has the same maze of corridors, enclosures, and towers, but has been better preserved. Built by Jayavarman VII, it was dedicated in 1191 to 515 divinities and was a major center of worship, with eighteen major festivals taking place each year. The whole complex covers a large area. The temple itself is surrounded by a long wall approached by four processional walkways flanked by balustrades representing the Churning of the Sea of Milk; many of the figures are headless. Four vaulted corridors enter the central sanctuary from the four cardinal points. Many finely carved images remain, including those of *apsaras* and *essais* (sages). Entry is from the west gate. Look out for the Grecian-looking

A view of the exterior at Banteay Srei Temple.

two-story building inside the east gate, which remains
something of a mystery.

Banteay Srei

Dedicated to Shiva, Banteay Srei (Citadel of Women) is
the most delicate and beautiful of the temples at Angkor.
Built of pinkish stone, the carving is as fine and delicate
as any to be found anywhere. Construction began in 967
and was commissioned by a Brahman who may have
been a tutor to Jayavarman V. The building is square and
is approached from the east by a causeway. The carvings
represent male and female deities and scenes from the
Hindu epic Ramayana. Almost every surface of the
interior is covered with decoration. This is one temple
that must be seen to view Khmer art at its finest and
most beautiful.

CHAPTER EIGHT

BUSINESS BRIEFING

Cambodia's economy is growing, though it is still hampered by the effects of the years of conflict and the policies of the Pol Pot regime. Exports grew 23 percent during 2021, while garment sector exports increased by 15.2 percent. Banking and financial structures are being reformed and developed, and much has been done to restore and improve the country's infrastructure. The port of Sihanoukville has been enlarged and modernized, while the development of new and existing airports will help to increase the number of visitors to Cambodia, in line with an expected increase in tourism following the coronavirus pandemic. In further infrastructure developments, the railway has been expanded and the road from Phnom Penh to Kampot has been widened. A new road between Phnom Penh to Sihanoukville has been built, and work continues on important roadways throughout the country.

Cambodia has received injections of aid and investment from numerous international sources. In 2017, Prime Minister Hun Sen led a large delegation to attend the first Belt and Road Forum in Beijing that saw China pledge US $240 million in grants to Cambodia. Both countries signed thirteen agreements focusing on a wide range of areas including infrastructure development, production capacity, trade, finance, maritime cooperation, and tourism under the Belt and Road framework. The authorities believe that this will encourage economic development and regional integration and connectivity.

Cambodia's textile industry has been a success, though it is now facing tougher competition, especially from China. Cambodia saw its dream of becoming the eighth oil producer among the ten members of ASEAN falter when Singapore-based KrisEnergy, which operates the Apsara oil field in the Gulf of Thailand off Sihanoukville, announced in 2021 that it had filed for liquidation. The company said at the time that it was unable to repay its debts.

The construction sector has done well in recent years, largely due to Chinese investment. The Cambodian government actively encourages foreign enterprise and investment, and companies and firms with thorough proposals are welcomed. The government is anxious to improve the education and skills of the population, so training schemes to develop the skills of Cambodian management and workers are a focus. Also, projects that require local representatives or partners are prime as they can relate to the way Cambodians do business.

Nongovernmental Organizations (NGOs) play a significant role in Cambodia's development by channeling foreign aid into sectors such as education, medical and health services, welfare programs, assisting small businesses, and tackling social problems. They provide employment, expertise, and training, and aim at increasing Cambodia's self-sufficiency and ability to sustain improved standards of living. NGOs can represent a relatively efficient and cost-effective use of aid while providing training and employment. It is common for travelers to volunteer to work for an NGO in exchange for food and accommodation. Doing this is a good way to maximize your experience in Cambodia while living on a budget. The Web site Workaway has a large selection of volunteering opportunities all over the Kingdom. Simply register online and have a look at the options.

BUSINESS CULTURE

Business in Cambodia is based on the same core Asian values underpinning the business cultures of its neighbors, namely respect, hierarchy, networking, consensus, and nonconfrontation. In such a culture personal contact is important, and the higher up the hierarchy the more influential they will be. If you are planning to do business in Cambodia or with Cambodians, try to establish personal contact with someone who can introduce you to the people you will need to see in government and business circles, as a good contact can prove invaluable. It is also important to learn the language if you want to gain trust and respect from locals.

If you are assigned to Cambodia to work in an enterprise that is already established, your status will depend on your position in the hierarchy. You will become aware that interaction between yourself and Cambodian colleagues and staff within the office will be more formal than you are accustomed to, although younger people with some Western experience may be more relaxed. It is important to find out the ages and positions held of the people you are working with so that you may treat them with the appropriate respect.

Watch the Time
To avoid confusion about time, use the twenty-four-hour clock for making appointments and arranging meetings. When writing dates, Cambodians use the system common throughout the region of day/month/year: 14/4/2022 for April 14, 2022. To avoid confusion, it is advisable to use the full date in correspondence and to reconfirm meetings and appointments in advance.

OFFICE ETIQUETTE AND PROTOCOL

As a foreigner employed in an office you will likely be in a position of some authority, although, depending on the type of business and its size, you may have Cambodians in positions higher in the hierarchy. Within the office, it is important to show respect to those senior to yourself and also to those who are senior in years. Any differences of opinion or any criticism must be conveyed in indirect and respectful terms. Similarly, you can expect respectful behavior from those below you in the corporate structure, but in return treat them with consideration and respect. If there are failings, deal with them diplomatically and not in public. A confrontation would be counterproductive, and it is you who would lose face and respect.

MANAGEMENT STYLE

Management in the private sector has been influenced by French corporate structures. There is usually a director-general, followed by a general manager, and then managers. Occasionally, a president may rank above the director-general. You will have a position in this hierarchy and should recognize the responsibilities you have to those above and below you in the hierarchy. Remember that, whatever the managerial structure of the business and the office, a confrontational approach will be self-defeating. However, you are entitled to the respect of those below you in the management structure and those younger in years.

MEETINGS AND GREETINGS

You will encounter a mixture of traditional and Western behavior. As described earlier in the book, Cambodians traditionally greet each other with a *sompeah*, which involves placing the palms of the hands together, raising to the chest, and bowing slightly. You may still see such greetings at meetings and conferences, particularly among older participants or when a younger person meets an older person. However, the Western handshake has become the usual practice between men, although women usually continue to exchange the traditional greeting between themselves. Foreigners should shake the hands of both men and women, although you should wait until the woman extends her hand before extending your own. If she does not, a slight bow will show courtesy and respect.

On the first meeting with Cambodians with whom you may be conducting business, greet the highest-ranking person first. If you are in a group, the most senior member of your group should greet the most senior member of the other. Other members should be introduced in hierarchical order and using any titles that indicate academic achievement (such as "Doctor," for instance) and their position in your organization or delegation (chairman, project manager, personal assistant), so that both sides understand the levels of authority. When addressing your Cambodian counterparts, use their titles until you are informed otherwise. If you have not noted their titles and rank in previously written information sent to you, their business cards will contain that information.

It is not polite to get straight down to business. Meetings should begin with casual conversation—about your journey to the meeting, recent events, your impressions of the country, and so on. Keep your remarks favorable and uncritical. You may be offered some tea, a soft drink, or water. Sometimes business meetings are even preceded with some alcoholic beverages to loosen the tension. It is polite to take a few sips, but not necessary to drink it all. If you do, it is likely to be refilled. This preamble is to enable everyone to size each other up and to form first impressions.

A meeting will have been set up for a particular length of time. Ascertain what time has been allocated for it, especially if dealing with a person in the government or bureaucracy, but also if with a business contact. Your Cambodian counterpart will be reluctant to take the initiative to end the meeting, as that would be bad manners. As the guest you should make the move when the time allocated has ended.

BUSINESS CARDS

Carry enough business cards to hand to all present, beginning with the most senior member of the group. You should have your card printed in Khmer on one side and English on the other. Offer the card with both hands, or the right hand. If the card is printed in Khmer, present it with the Khmer side up. When offered a card accept it with both hands or the right hand and a slight inclination of the head. The way you treat the card is indicative of your respect for the person presenting it.

NEGOTIATIONS

As the meeting and business discussions develop, be polite, and be careful to avoid confrontation. An agreement may not be reached, but differences can be made clear without creating conflict, as face-saving is important for both sides. Proposals from the Cambodian side will be cautiously worded and put forward as suggestions, while silence is an indication of disagreement, which will not be openly stated. Negotiations, therefore, take the form of probing by both sides to arrive at a consensus.

The negotiation process is not merely a matter of language. Cambodians conceal anger and frustration, often behind a smile that may indicate incomprehension, disagreement, nervousness, or irritation. Also bear in mind that your counterpart may not be able to commit to any decision at the time of your meeting, but may have to report progress to a superior.

The Cambodian approach may appear frustrating or indecisive to those used to doing business in the West, but speaking frankly and forcibly, being bombastic and boastful, or expressing frustration and anger will be counterproductive. From the Cambodian perspective, you will have lost face and also their respect for what they consider bad manners and a lack of control.

Younger colleagues and subordinates who have overseas experience are likely to fall in with Western management styles more easily than people without such experience. On the other hand, the latter is likely to have knowledge and understanding of and links into the bureaucracy and existing management systems. Their advice and experience should be treated with respect, and any changes introduced with regard to their views and feelings.

SPEECHES AND PRESENTATIONS

The basic organization of an event where you may need to give a speech or presentation will likely be much as you are used to. In most cases, you will have access to familiar audiovisual and computer-assisted programs. PowerPoint presentations with the employment of visual images, charts, diagrams, and graphs can help an audience, not all of whom may be fluent in English, to understand you. The inclusion of videos is also extremely helpful and engaging. However, the situation will be formal, and people mentioned in the presentation or spoken to from the platform should be addressed according to title and rank. Such public events are often arranged to present a consensus arrived at beforehand through negotiations with interested parties and their intermediaries.

If you are delivering your speech or presentation in English to an audience containing people not fully conversant with the language, you should speak clearly and slowly, avoid jargon, and explain concepts clearly.

Interpreters

If necessary, employ an interpreter. If you are presenting concepts, information, and views that may be challenged, or that may affect the interests of members of the audience, it would be wise to employ your own interpreter rather than one supplied by an organization with its own agenda. Remember to concentrate on those you are addressing— you should avoid the temptation to turn to or to address the interpreter. However, also avoid prolonged eye contact, which can be interpreted as aggressive.

BUREAUCRACY AND CORRUPTION

Although they operate like private enterprises, most modern Cambodian businesses are public entities. Each province in the country is governed by a local political leader, and corruption is widespread, particularly in the public sector. Access to timber concessions is one area where corruption has been rife, but there are other segments of the economy where individual enterprises benefit from their connections with government officials. Cambodia received a low ranking from Transparency International in 2020—160 out of 180 countries—and 37 percent of public service users reported to have paid a bribe in that same year. The government is attempting to tackle the problem, but it is prevalent at all levels.

Because of the emphasis on personal dealings within business relationships, it is necessary to ascertain, as far as possible, the status and connections of those with whom you are hoping to do business. Be wary of those who would place you under an obligation by proffering lavish gifts and hospitality. If you are offered such hospitality or gifts, either politely decline or reciprocate to an equal degree, and thus retain your status.

WOMEN IN BUSINESS

Women are particularly important in the business sector. Most small businesses and privately owned shops are staffed by women, while large firms often employ

A media interview with Cambodian-American entrepreneur Maya Gilliss-Chapman, CEO of Cambodians in Tech.

female office staff and secretaries, some of whom attain important executive positions, although the higher levels of management are predominantly male.

WORKING WITHIN THE SYSTEM

Working or conducting business in Cambodia requires patience and understanding of the traditions and practices that affect relations within the workplace, between business contacts, and between those business contacts and government officials. However, Cambodians are moving away from the trauma of conflict and as the economy modernizes and expands, and business and commercial opportunities and contacts grow, relations become easier. Nevertheless, the underlying culture remains and it is wise to conform to it until you are sure of your position in it. Every year you will need to purchase a work permit if you are employed or self-employed in Cambodia. These can be arranged at visa offices and you will need proof of your employment. If you are caught working without a permit you will be penalized.

BLESSING THE PROJECT

When a project is begun, or a new building or office is opened, your Cambodian colleagues may suggest that it should be blessed in a ceremony conducted by monks. The ceremony requires sitting on the floor while the monks seated opposite chant and say prayers, after which they are ceremoniously fed. The whole event may last for over two hours, during which you must be seated in the lotus position or with your legs tucked to one side. If you are not used to sitting in this position, it may be possible to have a low platform constructed upon which the monks may sit. This way you could sit on a cushion without raising your head above theirs, which would be offensive. It may also be suggested that the new building should have a spirit house, in which case seek the advice of your Cambodian colleagues.

CHAPTER NINE

COMMUNICATING

LANGUAGE

Khmer is the official language of Cambodia, but some level of English and French are also spoken by many who have been to school. English is increasingly important in business, so if you have come to Cambodia for work, you will find that the majority of those you work with will have some command of it—often a very good command—and will usually be happy to use it. French is a useful subsidiary language that many older Khmers will have learned. The most influential linguistic development of recent years is the rise in people speaking Chinese, both locals and foreigners. The Confucius Institute was first opened in Cambodia in 2009 and today runs hundreds of classes all over the country teaching Chinese language, culture, and customs. With many Chinese businesses in Cambodia, the stated goal of the institute is to improve the job prospects of its local students and according to the

institute, many of its students have been recruited by the Chinese government and the Chinese Embassy in Cambodia.

Speaking English

Cambodians have not been slow to recognize the advantages of learning English. English is the language of tourism and commerce, and English language schools operate throughout the country. Many of the teachers may not themselves be fluent in English, but the demand is there. You will find that many of the Cambodians you meet will be anxious to practice their English with you, even if their grasp is only very basic. It is a good opportunity to build rapport and to learn some Khmer in return.

Khmer

Learning some Khmer has many advantages, even if you'll only be in the country for a short period of time. Beyond practical utility, using a few basic phrases goes a long way to express an interest in and respect for Cambodian culture, something that will not be lost on your hosts.

Khmer has its roots in Sanskrit and Pali and has been influenced by contacts with the languages of its neighbors and, during the colonial period, by French, which introduced many technical and medical terms. Unlike the languages of its neighbors, Khmer is nontonal, but it has a complex system of thirty-three consonants and twenty-three vowels. Transliteration into the Roman alphabet under the French can make language learning easier, though achieving correct pronunciation using transliteration only is tricky. Transliteration is also not uniform, so expect variation in different Khmer language guides.

While pronunciation can be difficult, Khmer grammar is relatively simple. There are no verb conjugations and no different endings for singular, plural, masculine, or feminine nouns. Instead, changes in tense are conveyed by the use of particles.

FORMS OF ADDRESS

As will be clear by now, social standing and politeness are critical components of Cambodian society. As such, it's important to use the correct forms of address based on the age and social position of the person you are talking to. As a foreigner, you will be forgiven for not knowing all the requisite forms of address, but the following advice will be helpful.

Niak (you) may be used in most situations and with either sex.

Lok (Mister) may be used for men of your own age or older.

Lok srei (Madam) is a formal address for women of your age or older.

Bong is a convenient neutral pronoun for men or women who are, or appear to be, older than you.

Bong srei (older sister) may be used for less formal occasions.

Koat is the respectful form of the third person singular or plural for men or women. The common form is *ke*.

If you stay in the country long enough to make close friends, you may be invited to use the family-oriented forms of address mentioned in Chapter Two. Until then, it's best to err on the side of formality and respect.

FACE-TO-FACE

In addition to using the appropriate terms of address, it's important to avoid behavior that may cause a loss of face, either to yourself or your interlocutor. For example, in order to save face, the person you're talking to may prefer to tell you what they think you want to hear, rather than what is actually the case. If you are unsure, rather than press them on the matter, which would also cause them to lose face, pay attention to nuances of voice and behavior, and bear in mind that the true situation may only later be revealed by intermediaries, and even then perhaps only in guarded terms. Your ability to pick up on behavioral nuances will improve with time, and your ability to be more frank without causing undue offense will increase the more you get to know someone.

In conversation, be sure to speak clearly and to avoid colloquialisms and slang that non-native English speakers will be unfamiliar with. Many Cambodians can speak English proficiently, but others will be less confident and liable to mishear or misunderstand. Conversely, it may take you time to become accustomed to the nuances of Cambodian-spoken English. If you need to ask someone to repeat a statement, do so politely, perhaps with some deprecatory remark about your hearing or understanding.

HUMOR

Cambodians possess a sense of humor and respond to the ridiculous. Slapstick comedy in particular is popular, though in a society where maintaining face is paramount, one should refrain from laughing at people in real life. Jokes made at another's expense will take place in theatrical performance, and much to the audience's enjoyment, but in personal relations there is a fine line between what may be humorous and what produces shame, so tread carefully. At times, a laugh or smile may also be an indication that a person has not fully understood what you have said and is an attempt to cover embarrassment. On the other hand, as a foreigner, you will likely make humorous mistakes. When it does

Women relaxing and conversing in the relative cool of the evening.

happen, your Cambodian acquaintances may be too polite to laugh or comment, but if you can laugh or smile at your errors, they will be delighted that you are not embarrassed and will laugh or smile with you.

BODY LANGUAGE

Body language is important, especially when verbal communication may be difficult. A rough manner is regarded as offensive, and the perpetrator as boorish and rude. Your posture and demeanor should indicate respect and reserve. How you sit or stand may convey respect and dignity, or aggression and bad manners. Thus, don't stand with one or both hands in your pockets or on your hips, which indicates disrespect and arrogance. Instead, clasp your hands lightly in front of you, as this shows respect. When sitting, it is disrespectful to lean back with legs outstretched or to sit with them crossed or parted. To pat a person on the back is also a sign of disrespect, especially if that person is older or in a senior position.

To point at someone is considered rude, and to jab a finger at someone while making a point in an argument would be considered offensive. If it is necessary to catch someone's attention, or summon them, use the whole hand to beckon, with the palm turned down. To summon with the finger and the palm turned up is an offensive gesture. If it is necessary to point, use the thumb only.

Facial gestures such as grimacing, pouting, and winking are also considered impolite and should be avoided in any formal setting.

These general rules of conduct may appear relatively insignificant, but in a society where age and seniority carry respect, they can make a great difference to how one is perceived. If you develop good relations with Cambodians, then the formality may be relaxed, especially in private, but in public or a professional environment, it is necessary to show respect.

CELL PHONES AND SIM CARDS

Cell phones are as ubiquitous in Cambodia today as they are in the rest of the world and it is advisable to purchase a local SIM card if you are planning on being in the country for anything longer than a couple of weeks, and even for short-term travel it can be very handy. Cambodia has one of the most competitive mobile markets in the world and so the price of SIM cards and data packages are low. SIM cards can be purchased on arrival at the airport or at any of the many phone shops around the country. Network carriers are required to keep a copy of your passport on file, but many of the small shops don't bother with this requirement. If you lose your phone, however, you can get a replacement SIM if your passport was registered at the time of purchase. The network providers that offer the best coverage are Cellcard, Metfone, and Smart. The Cambodian country code is +855.

INTERNET

Connectivity in Cambodia is developing rapidly. In 2021, approximately 53 percent of Cambodians had access to the Internet, which represented a 14 percent increase on the previous year alone. In 2009, that figure was at less than 1 percent.

In cities, Wi-Fi is readily available at many hotels, cafés, restaurants, and shops, but can be harder to find on the islands and in rural areas, where connection speeds may also be slow. Internet cafés also provide cheap access to the Internet but are becoming less common as mobile penetration increases.

Internet users should be aware that the government conducts widespread surveillance and censorship of online content.

SOCIAL MEDIA

The age of social media and the emoji epidemic has well and truly hit most ASEAN countries, among them Cambodia, where by 2021 more than 71 percent of the population were using social media, an increase of 24 percent on the previous year. Facebook, YouTube, TikTok, and Instagram are Cambodia's favorite social media platforms, and not just by the young. Facebook, for example, is a very popular resource for news and current affairs, businesses, and social activism. Not all businesses will have tailored websites, but they will almost certainly have a Facebook presence.

MAIL

Generally speaking, the postal service in Cambodia is reliable. Each town has a post office and there are many in Phnom Penh, though depending on where you are, you may have to pick up a package or mail at the post office as postcodes can cover entire provinces. It is advisable to send important or valuable items by one of the international courier services, which have offices in all major cities. Reliable companies include Virak Buntham, Larryta, and Mekong Express. If you send mail over the counter at a post office, ensure that the items are franked before you leave.

THE MEDIA

Cambodia had a relatively independent press during and immediately following the UNTAC era—a United Nations peacekeeping operation that was set up after the 1991 Paris Peace Accords. Prime Minister Hun Sen and his party, the CPP, have since come to strictly control media in Cambodia. This has more recently encompassed social media, which surpassed traditional media as a news source for Cambodians in 2017. In 2020 the prime minister said he gave reporters "magic powers to extend their professionalism, gain trust from the public and defend themselves before the law." But to make the most of the powers, he cautioned journalists not to "violate the right of others and don't distort the truth."

According to the Ministry of Information, there are over 460 print outlets registered in Cambodia. However, the Ministry considers only fifty of them as active. Among the most relevant print outlets, half of them belong to politically affiliated owners, according to Media Ownership Monitor, an affiliate of Reporters without Borders.

Four outlets dominate—*The Koh Santepheap Daily*, *The Phnom Penh Post*, *The Cambodia*, and

The Southeast Asia Weekly Daily—but only 11 percent of Cambodians read either a magazine or a newspaper regularly. Many newspapers and private radio and television stations are run by political parties or individual politicians which is reflected in their coverage.

Newspapers

The main English-language newspapers in Cambodia are the *Phnom Penh Post* and the *Khmer Times*, while the most widely circulated Khmer-language newspapers are *Reaksmei Kampuchea* and *Kaoh Santepheap* (both pro-government dailies). The national news agency is Agence Kampuchea Presse (AKP). According to the director of Cambodia Journalist Alliance, press freedom in Cambodia has been in steady decline since 2017, and in 2021 was ranked 144th in the world. That same year, the *Khmer Times* stated that 95 percent of journalists expressed concern over corruption-related information being published. According to CamboJA, the Covid-19 pandemic was used by the government to restrict the dissemination of information.

Radio and Television

Television is the most popular media type in Cambodia, reaching 96 percent of the population. According to the Ministry of Information, Cambodia counts 18 TV stations. They include one state-owned TV station where viewership is lower than 1 percent. Eight of the nine relevant TV channels belong to owners who are politically affiliated to the ruling party. There is no official standard for media measurement used by the industry, other than self-promotional claims.

Radio has become less popular with the rise of the Internet. Nationally, it is now ranked as the third most important media sector after TV and Internet, and is used by only some 35 percent of the population. There are two AM stations and at least sixty-five FM radio stations in Cambodia. Advertising on the radio in Cambodia is relatively inexpensive. The main radio stations in Cambodia include: ABC Cambodia FM 107.5, Bayon Radio, Deum Ampil Radio, Mohachun FM 95.3, Mongkul, Sovann, Radio Free Asia, RFI FM 92, Sambok Khmom FM 105.

CONCLUSION

Cambodia has passed through a long and, at times, tumultuous history, overshadowed by the terrible events that took place between 1975 and 1979 under the ruthless regime of Pol Pot and the Khmer Rouge. The experiences of those years live on in memories and monuments.

Proud of their ancient culture and long traditions, and anxious to retain their sense of identity, the Cambodian people have rebuilt their country with strength and determination, to take its place among the modern nations of the world. Cambodia welcomes visitors with all the warmth, charm, and hospitality that its people possess in abundance.

USEFUL WORDS AND PHRASES

There is no commonly accepted form of transliteration from Khmer—with its thirty-three consonants and twenty-three vowels—into English, and publications on Cambodia vary. The following transliterations are kept as simple as possible to produce spoken sounds that a Cambodian is likely to understand.

Hello: *Chum reeup sooa* (formal) *Susaday* (informal)
Good-bye: *Chum reeup lear* (formal) *Lear hauwee* (informal)
Please: *Sohm*
Thank you: *Aw kohn*
Excuse me / I'm sorry: *Sohm toh*
Yes: *Baat* (used by men) *Jaas* (used by women)
No: *Tay*
I: *K'nyom*
You: *Niak*
I don't understand: *K'nyom s'dap men baan*
Can you speak English? *Niak jehs nit-yaly par sar Onglai?*
Lavatory: *Bong-kun*
Where is…? *…. now ain nar?*
Come: *Mow*
Go: *Toa*
What is your . . . ? *Niak . . . ai?*
What is your name? *Niak ch-moo-ah ai?*
Where are you going? *Tow nar?*
I am going to . . . *K'nyom tow . . .*
I want to go to . . . *K'nyom chong tow . . .*
Where is the . . . ? *. . . now ai nar?*
I am not well: *K'nyom men su-rooel kloo un tay*
I am lost: *K'nom vung-veing plaow*
How much does it cost? *Telai pon maan?*
Very expensive: *Telai nahs*
What is your best price? *Dait pon maan?*
Morning: *l pruk*
Noon: *T'ngai terong*

Afternoon: *Pel rohsiel*
Evening: *Pel l'ingiat*
Night: *Pel yop*
Day: *T'ingai*
Today: *T'ingai nee*
Tomorrow: *T'ingai sa-ait*
Yesterday: *M'sell-mine*
Hour: *Maung*
What is the time? *Maung pon maan?*

Numerals
0 *sohn*
1 *moi*
2 *pee*
3 *bei*
4 *boun*
5 *bram*
6 *bram-moi*
7 *bram-pee*
8 *bram-bei*
9 *bram-boun*
10 *duop*
11 *duop-moi*
12 *duop-pee*

Some words have been adopted into Khmer from French or English, for example *pohs poli*, (police station), *ohtel* (hotel), *taksee* (taxi), and *restoran* (restaurant).

USEFUL APPS

Communication
The most popular social media and communication apps in Cambodia are: **Telegram**, **Facebook**, **LINE**, **WeChat**, **Snapchat**, **Viber**, **WhatsApp**, **Skype**, **TikTok**, and **Twitter**. For translation and language learning use: **Simply Learn Cambodian**, **Ling**, **Vocly**, and **Learn To Write Khmer Alphabet**.

Travel & Transportation
PassApp – A popular ride-hailing app for tuk tuks and taxis throughout Cambodia. **Grab Taxi** – Most popular app for transport in Phnom Penh. **WeGO**, **Eagle-App**, **SmartRide Cambodia**, **Zelo Taxi** – also useful for booking tuk tuks and taxis, predominantly operational in Phnom Penh and Siem Reap.

Food & Shopping
NHAM24 – groceries, meals, and pharmaceuticals, all delivered within 30 minutes in Phnom Penh, Siem Reap, Kampot, and Battambang. **E-GetS** – grocery and food delivery in Phnom Penh and Sihanoukville. **Food Panda** – groceries, meals, and pharmaceuticals delivered in all major cities. **Meal Temple** – food delivery service in Phnom Penh, Siem Reap, Battambang, and Sihanoukville. **TukOut** – food delivery service in Phnom Penh, Siem Reap, Sihanoukville, Battambang, Kampot, and Kep. Shop online with **Lazada**, **L192**, **PIIK MALL**, and **AliExpress**.

Banking
ABA Bank is an essential app for expats in Cambodia; it is the easiest to use for online banking. If you don't have an account with ABA, **Wing** is the most reliable app for payment in Cambodia, where you can deposit cash, book bus tickets, or top up your phone. **ACLEDA Mobile** is also used for online banking.

FURTHER READING

Brinkley, Joel. *Cambodia's Curse: The Modern History of a Troubled Land*. New York: PublicAffairs, 2012.

Chandler, David P. *A History of Cambodia*. Chiang Mai, Thailand: 1998; Boulder, Colorado; and Oxford: Westview Press, 2000.

Chandler, David P. *Brother Number One: A Political Biography of Pol Pot*. Chiang Mai, Thailand: Silkworm Books, 1999.

Jessup, Helen. *Art and Architecture in Cambodia*. London: Thames & Hudson, 1994.

Ngor, Haing. *Survival in the Killing Fields*. New York: Basic Books, 2003.

Osborne, Lewis. *Sihanouk. Prince of Light, Peace of Darkness*. St. Leonards: Allen & Unwin, 1994.

Philpotts, Robert. *The Coast of Cambodia*. London: Blackwater Books, 2001.

Ponchaud, Francois. *Cambodia Year Zero*, Harmondsworth: Penguin, 1978.

Pym, Christopher (ed.) (abridged). *Henri Mouhot's Diary, Travels in the Central Plains of Siam, Cambodia and Laos During the Years 1858-61*. Kuala Lumpur: Oxford University Press, 1966.

Ray, Nick. *Cambodia*. Hawthorn, Victoria; Oakland, California; London; and Paris: Lonely Planet Publications, 2005.

Ros, Rotanak. *NHUM: Recipes from a Cambodian Kitchen*. Rotanak Food Media, 2019.

Shawcross, William. *Sideshow: Kissinger, Nixon, and the Destruction of Cambodia*. Lanham: Cooper Square Press, 2002.

Strangio, Sebastian. *Cambodia: From Pol Pot to Hun Sen and Beyond*. New Haven: Yale University Press, 2020.

Szymusiak, Molyda (trans. Linda Coverdale). *The Stones Cry Out. A Cambodian Childhood, 1975-80*. London: Jonathan Cape, 1987.

PICTURE CREDITS

INDEX

Acknowledgements

With special thanks to Raphael, whose knowledge and understanding of Cambodian culture and tradition have been invaluable.